Incarnate Spirits

An Introduction to Philosophical Anthropology

To Tim,
May this book lead you to a deeper understanding of human beings, yourself, & Notre Dame football!
—Fr. Derick
11/12/20[illegible]

Incarnate Spirits

An Introduction to Philosophical Anthropology

Roderrick Esclanda

Published by Scepter Publishers, Inc.
info@scepterpublishers.org
www.scepterpublishers.org
800-322-8773
New York

Cover Image: Adam and Eve Naïve Paintings, Kalacha, Kenya. Alamy stock photo.
Cover Design: Studio Red Design
Page Design and Composition: Rose Design

Library of Congress Control Number: 2023948922

ISBN paperback: 978-1-59417-521-3
ISBN eBook: 978-1-59417-522-0

Printed in the United States of America

CONTENTS

INTRODUCTION

Questions

In Terrence Malick's *The Thin Red Line*, we find this brief exchange:

> **First Sgt. Edward Welsh (played by Sean Penn):** "In this world, a man himself is nothing. And there ain't no world but this one."
>
> **Private Witt (played by Jim Caviezel):** "You're wrong, there, Top: I've seen another world. Sometimes I think it was just my imagination."
>
> **Welsh:** "Well, then you've seen things I never will."

This interchange draws our attention to a truth unique to human persons: the fact that we are both bodily as well as spiritual beings. On the one hand, we live, like other animals, in the world as beings that experience reality through our bodies, with our senses, and with our feelings; that is, we are embodied beings. On the other hand, unlike all other animals, we are aware of being in the world, we are conscious of being aware, we pose questions, and we at times experience a deep sense that there is something beyond this world; that is, we are spiritual beings. And yet, a human being is not a combination of two separate beings (a body plus a spirit), but rather one substantial unity of body and soul. We are spiritual beings, but not separate spirits that come to dwell in bodies. We are, instead, *incarnate spirits*. As incarnate spirits, we are material beings with an inner personal intimacy.

A hallmark of Terrence Malick films is the prevalent use of an off-camera voice when we hear the protagonist thinking and pondering. Its use is not simply expository: it is not merely filling in some contextual hole that requires explanation. The character's voice, instead, makes us privy to her innermost thoughts and feelings to which those outside her intimacy would be completely oblivious. But hearing someone's inner voice allows us to enter even more deeply into a person's heart, to share not only someone's thoughts but also to experience, in some mysterious way, the heart and the intimacy of this person. The result is not only knowledge of the characteristics or traits of a person, or an insight into her actions or thoughts or feelings; instead, we come to know *who* she is. We enter, in some way, into the mystery of her intimacy. And as we do so, we begin to ask fundamental questions: What is a human person? Who is she? What is life? What does it mean to live in the world? What makes human beings different from other animals? What is reason? What is a soul? What is freedom? What happens when we die? Who are we? Who am I? What is my destiny?

These are questions that reverberate throughout human culture and history. They are also questions we pose to ourselves when alone, perhaps at the most random moments.

This little book is designed as an introductory guide for those who find themselves asking these questions. And to make things as simple as possible, we can reduce this to two questions: What is a human being? and Who am I?

More than simply giving quick and easy answers to these questions, this book offers a basic framework around which you, the reader, can begin to build habits and structures of thought that will enable you to personally grapple with these questions. It will also help you engage others and encourage them to do the same, as you, together with them, embark upon a lifelong journey of inquiry and discovery.

Philosophical Anthropology

The main perspective of this book is a philosophical one. By *philosophical*, we mean a *rational inquiry into the explanations (principles and causes) of realities*. Insofar as the area of our interests concerns human beings and to the extent that it is an introduction, this book is an introduction to *philosophical anthropology*.

The emphasis on a philosophical point of view distinguishes this introduction methodologically from (but does not completely separate it from) other modalities of wisdom (mythology, artistic insight, divine revelation, and so on), insofar as it seeks answers to fundamental questions using *rational inquiry* without depending directly on divinely revealed truths. This does not, however, mean that we will completely ignore other sources of knowledge, especially that of Christian revelation, since a complete answer to the kinds of questions we are asking can ultimately only be answered by God.

Our Guides

The questions that we are exploring in this book are wide-ranging and have been the object of inquiry for centuries, not only in the West but in every other culture as well. It is thus possible to go in many directions and to follow many paths, or even to make our own. In this book, however, we will take a well-trodden (yet still exciting) philosophical path.

The specific type of philosophical anthropology that will be a map for our journey is one that is based on Aristotelian-Thomistic philosophy. This philosophy, with its origins in Aristotle (fourth-century BC Greece) and Thomas Aquinas (thirteenth-century Western Europe), has for centuries been a central and organizing principle of Western philosophical and theological thought. Later chapters will supplement this map with philosophical insights from contemporary thinkers, especially Joseph Ratzinger, Karol Wojtyła, and Leonardo Polo.

The choice to take Aquinas as our guiding and structuring philosopher arises from a number of considerations.

First, Aquinas' philosophy introduces us to key philosophical notions that are crucial for any in-depth inquiry into the nature of human beings. This includes notions such as soul, corporality, substance, power, operation, object, habit, ends, and means.

Second, Aquinas offers an expansive yet structured view of human nature. Aristotle and Aquinas (with considerations from medieval Islamic philosophers) have developed an anthropology that is both comprehensive and minutely detailed. Aquinas lays out and describes a wide range of powers that are found in human beings. These powers or capabilities range from the most basic (the powers of nourishment, growth, and reproduction) to more elaborate ones (such as the external senses, the powers by which we organize sense perceptions and evaluate them, the powers to respond emotionally to sense stimuli) to those that are most spiritual (reason and free will). At the same time, this description is filled with detailed accounts of the various operations and vital activities that make up human life: eating, seeing color, smelling roses, feeling joy or pain, making saddles, scientific knowledge, moral action, growing in virtue, seeking happiness, and much more.

Third, since Aristotelian-Thomistic philosophy has been so central to Western thought, a familiarity with its basic elements and language will unlock for the reader an immense treasure-trove of philosophical thought from the past and the present.

And finally, having a basic map that helps us understand human nature and its dynamism allows us to critically and creatively engage with questions of special relevance in today's world. Questions, for example, that concern the difference between animal and human intelligence, artificial intelligence, gender, and personal identity.

The Structure of This Book

Broadly speaking, this book has two parts.

The first part covers the basic structure of the human person based on an Aristotelian-Thomistic framework. The first eight chapters lay out the essential elements of this anthropology: life and the soul (chapter 1); the organic body and the notions of powers and operations (chapter 2); sense knowledge (chapter 3); feelings (chapter 4); intellect and reason (chapter 5); the will (chapter 6); science and craft (chapter 7); and moral action and virtue (chapter 8).

Chapters 9 and 10 add contemporary elements to the Aristotelian-Thomistic anthropology covered in the first eight chapters. Chapter 9 considers human subjectivity and the person as gift-love. Chapter 10 expands this perspective to manifestations of the person in the world and with other human persons.

Advice on How to Read this Book

Finally, a word of advice (or warning) to you, the reader. Taking Aquinas as our guide and looking to authors such as Ratzinger, Wojtyła, and Polo for insights into human existence is not for the faint of heart. It will require serious attention and sustained focus. It is not an effort simply to understand complex notions and memorize vast amounts of information. Rather, it is an attention and focus directed at engaging with these guides in a conversation that demands that the reader actively engage the intellect and sometimes even the heart. Though at first seemingly daunting, it will enable us to take the first steps in a long-lasting and fruitful adventure of inquiry and wonder.

CHAPTER 1

Life and Soul

Life

Life and self-movement

A feature of Wampanoag (the language spoken by native peoples that the *Mayflower* settlers first encountered near what today is Plymouth, Massachusetts) is that nouns are classified according to whether they designate beings that are animate (as in, has spirit) or inanimate (does not have spirit). This distinction between animate and inanimate nouns gives rise to distinct grammatical features. The plural form of nouns, for example, depends on whether the noun is animate or inanimate. The plural of animate nouns is formed by adding the suffix *-ak* to the singular form. For example, the singular for "dog "is *anum*, and the plural is *anumwak*; the singular for "bear" is *masq*, and the plural is *masqak*. The plural form of inanimate nouns, on the other hand, is formed by adding the suffix *-ash* to the singular. For example: *apun* ("bed") and *apunash* ("beds"); *sapaheek* ("soup") and *sapaheekash* (soups). Interestingly enough, an indication that Wampanoag nouns do indeed designate living beings is that the animate plural suffix *-ak* continued to be used even when new European animals were introduced: *cowsak* ("cows"); *horseak* ("horses"); and *pigsak* ("pigs").

This classification of words assumes that Wampanoag speakers easily distinguish between animate and inanimate beings. We too easily distinguish living things from nonliving ones, and we do so from a very early age (even if we also sometimes encounter borderline cases such as viruses and prions). But what is the basis for these judgments? What is life? How do we know something is alive? Although we normally immediately know that something is alive when we see and observe it, we struggle to explain or define what exactly life is.

A dog is obviously alive. But a rock (even if I call it my "pet rock") is not. Perhaps we say a dog is alive because it does things that show that it is alive: it barks, it looks around, and it engages with the environment that surrounds it. I, too, seem to be alive (I seem to do the same sort of thing dogs do, although I don't normally bark). But what about the cactus plant? Is it alive? It doesn't bark, nor does it look around (or at least it doesn't seem to). Cacti do not seem to get up and move around from one place to another. And yet we say that cactus plants are alive. Perhaps this is because we do notice that cacti "do" things that living things do. For example, they seem to grow (albeit slowly), nourish themselves, and reproduce.

The rock, on the other hand, continues to sit around, not doing anything at all. True, it might be basking under the sun, and its temperature might increase, but it certainly doesn't seem actively to be doing anything with all that solar energy. Unlike the cactus plant, which seems to take the energy of sunlight and transform it for its own activity, the rock seems to just passively sit around, absorbing (but not doing anything with) the energy from the sun.

Then there's what rational, feeling, musical beings do with the sun, whether it be feeling "Sunshine on My Shoulders" (John Denver), exclaiming "Here Comes the Sun" (The Beatles), or proclaiming that "You Are My Sunshine" (Johnny Cash) or even that "You are the Sunshine of My Life" (Stevie

Wonder). Here, the sun, far from simply being a source of physical energy and sensation, becomes the source of new expressions of a deeper, more intimate life.

But back to our question. What, then, is life? Why do we identify something as alive and some other things as not alive? Thomas Aquinas asked these same questions, and his approach was to focus his attention first of all on those beings that most obviously seem to be alive, namely animals:

> Beginning with those things that clearly have life, we can determine which things have life and which do not. Now, life clearly belongs to animals; for *De Vegetabilibus* says, "Life is manifest in the animals." Hence, *we should distinguish living things from non-living things by looking at the reason why animals are said to have life*. But this will be whatever life is first manifested in and which remains to the last.[1]

Aquinas then homes in on what he thinks is most characteristic of animal life:

> Now we first say that an animal has life when it begins to have *movement from itself*, and an animal is judged to be alive for as long as such movement is apparent in it; and when it no longer has movement from itself, but is moved only by another, then an animal is said to be dead because of the absence of life. From this it is clear that *the things that have life in the proper sense are those that move themselves with some type of movement. . . .* Accordingly, *things*

1. Thomas Aquinas, *Summa Theologiae*, trans. Alfred J. Freddoso, "New English Translation of St. Thomas Aquinas' *Summa Theologiae*," updated July 11, 2023, https://www3.nd.edu/~afreddos/summa-translation/TOC.htm), 1.18.1, emphasis added.

> *that impel themselves to some sort of movement or action are said to have life*, whereas things whose nature is not such that they impel themselves to any movement or action cannot be said to have life.[2]

Aquinas, like us, is able to identify something as alive because it has "movement from itself." As we will see, these "movements," which are also called *vital operations*, can be of various sorts, including, but not limited to, taking nutriment, growing, sensation, and intellectual knowledge. When we observe something exercising one or more of these operations, we judge that it is alive. Oftentimes, this is obvious: a dog barks, sniffs, runs, eats, and fetches the newspaper. Sometimes, it requires closer attention: a cactus plant nourishes itself and grows, but slowly. When we fail to observe these kinds of movements in a thing, we judge that it is not alive. My pet rock, for example, is still sitting on the windowsill where I left it twelve years ago. So, although I might imagine that it could possibly be (in my wildest dreams) alive, I have to admit, thinking rationally about it, that it is not.

What is life?

We can easily tell when something is alive, and we do so quickly when we observe some sort of change or activity that comes from within the living being. But what *is* life?

The *Oxford English Dictionary* (American edition) defines life as "the condition that distinguishes animals and plants from inorganic matter," and it then goes on to give examples of this: "the capacity for growth, reproduction, functional activity, and continual change preceding death."

---

2. Aquinas, *Summa Theologiae* 1.18.1, emphasis added.

This definition, however, does not tell us what life itself is; it simply tells us that it is some sort of "condition." However, it does not explain what this condition consists in.

Here, Aquinas offers us an interesting insight. Instead of thinking of life as some sort of quality or property of living things, or as a separate entity that can be extracted or injected into bodies to make them alive, he considers two uses of the word *life*.

First, the word *life* designates "a *substance* which by its nature moves or impels itself in some way to an action."[3]

In other words, *life* designates the living substances themselves, and not just a quality.

Secondly, "sometimes the name 'life' is taken less properly for the *vital operations* from which the name 'life' was first taken."[4]

Aquinas is thus saying that the word *life* refers primarily to those beings (or substances) whose way of being (or nature) is to be alive. Secondarily, *life* refers to the kinds of activities that living beings exercise (which we have earlier called *vital operations* or self-movement).

This seems to be how we still use the word *life* today. We say, for example, that there is life in the ocean depths, and what we mean by this is that there are *living beings* that live in the deep ocean (and not just some sort of separate life force waiting to animate bodies to make them alive). Similarly, when we say that we are looking for life on Mars, we mean that we are looking for living *beings* on Mars that are identifiable as living by their *vital operations*.

3. Aquinas, *Summa Theologiae* 1.18.2, emphasis added.

4. Aquinas, *Summa Theologiae* 1.18.2, emphasis added.

Soul

Soul: the principle of life

Living beings are beings that move themselves; that is, they exercise vital operations. But what *makes* something alive? Or, phrased more philosophically, What is the principle of life in living things?

The classical answer comes to us through the ancient Greek philosophers, who distinguished living (or animate) beings from nonliving (inanimate) ones. For them, one was "animate" or "ensouled," and the other was not. In other words, it is "animation" or "soul" that makes a being alive, and this applies to all living beings (not just human beings, but also plants and nonhuman animals).

As Aquinas puts it, "a 'soul' (*anima*) is *a first principle of life in those things around us that are alive*; for we say that living things are 'ensouled' (*animata*) and that things which lack life are 'not ensouled' (*inanimata*)."[5]

Here, we have the basic answer to what makes a body alive: it is because it is an ensouled or animate body. We can, therefore, say that the soul is *the principle of life in living things.*

Soul: the substantial form of living beings

Now that we have identified the soul as the principle of life in living beings, we can push a bit more and ask just how a soul is a principle, and how it relates to the living being's physical body. To get a better understanding of this, though, it is necessary to introduce more technical vocabulary that may be initially difficult to understand. A good grasp of these terms is, however, fundamental to a deeper knowledge of living beings, and as

5. Aquinas, *Summa Theologiae* 1.75.1, emphasis added.

such, the time and effort needed to get a preliminary familiarity with them will be very much worth the effort.

Both Aristotle and Aquinas understand that living beings are *substances* and, more specifically, they are *physical bodies*. Now, some physical bodies are alive, while others are not.[6] A living body, then, is not just a body, but a *sort* of body; namely, a body that is alive. What makes a body that sort of body that is alive? For Aristotle and Aquinas, the answer cannot simply be that it is a body. After all, a rock is a body, but it is not, for that reason, a living body. Thus, the explanation for why one body is alive and another is not cannot simply be that they are bodies. To explain why a body is the sort of body that is alive, there needs to be another principle aside from the body; there must be a principle by which it is not just a body, but this *kind* of body, a *living* body.[7]

To understand what principle makes something to be a sort of body that is living, we need to look briefly at how Aristotle and Aquinas understand the principles of material beings in general. According to Aristotle and Aquinas, every material substance (including living beings) has both *matter* and *substantial form*. Matter is the physical stuff a material being is made out of, while substantial form is the immaterial principle that gives a being its specific nature or essence. The form is, therefore, what makes a thing *what* it is, and it organizes the

---

6. "Of natural bodies, some have life, while some do not have it." Aristotle, *De anima,* trans. C. D. C. Reeve (Indianapolis: Hackett, 2017), 2.1.412a13–14.

7. "For it is clear that being a *principle of life*, or *being alive* (*vivens*), cannot belong to a body by reason of its being a body; otherwise, each body would be alive or would be a principle of life. Therefore, the fact that a body is alive—or is even a principle of life—is something that belongs to it by virtue of the fact that it is a body of a given sort (*tale corpus*)." Aquinas, *Summa Theologiae* 1.75.1.

matter to be a specific kind or sort of substance. Thus, the principle that determines something to be a certain sort of thing is called its *substantial form*. This is true of both nonliving substances and ones that are alive.

Our modern chemical understanding of water, for example, tells us that water is composed, or made out, of hydrogen and oxygen. Therefore, we say that its "matter" (the stuff that it is made out of) is hydrogen and oxygen. Water, however, is not just hydrogen plus oxygen. We readily understand this if we consider that (under room temperature and pressure) hydrogen and oxygen are gases, but water is not. Instead, what we have when we put hydrogen and oxygen together in just the right way is a new kind of substance, namely, water, which is a liquid. Thus, water, although it is made out of hydrogen and oxygen, is not merely hydrogen plus oxygen, but rather a new compound or substance. What, then, explains what water is? From an Aristotelian perspective, it is not just the stuff or matter that water is made out of, but the substantial form of water.

This also explains why different kinds of substances can be made out of the same stuff yet be different kinds of things. Hydrogen peroxide, for example, is also made out of hydrogen and oxygen (more precisely, two hydrogen atoms and two oxygen atoms), and yet it is not water. It is some other *kind* of substance, namely hydrogen peroxide. Here, hydrogen peroxide is made out of the same stuff as water, and yet it is a different kind of thing. The difference, therefore, is not that water and hydrogen peroxide have different matter (they are both made out of hydrogen and oxygen); the difference is that they have different kinds of *substantial forms* that make them different *kinds* of things. Water is made out of hydrogen and oxygen, but it is water because of the substantial form of water. Hydrogen peroxide, too, is made out of hydrogen and oxygen, but it is hydrogen peroxide (and not water) because of the substantial form of hydrogen peroxide.

This explanatory analysis can be applied not only to inanimate substances but to living beings too. For example, a cactus plant and a dog may be made up out of similar stuff (organic molecules, proteins, and lipids), but they are different *sorts* of things: a cactus plant is a different *kind* of thing from a dog. What makes them different isn't the stuff that they are made out of, but their different substantial forms: a cactus is a cactus because it has the substantial form of a cactus plant; a dog is a dog because it has the substantial form of a dog.

Now, if we go back to our question about what makes a living being the sort of body that is living (a living one and not a nonliving one), we can understand why Aquinas says that this is because the stuff that the living body is made out of has a kind of substantial form that makes it precisely that sort of body that is living. To use our earlier examples, the substantial form of a cactus plant determines or configures the stuff that the cactus plant is made out of so that it is the living body of a cactus plant. The same can be said of a dog: a dog is a living body that is a dog because it has the substantial form of dog.

In short, we can say that living bodies are that sort of body because they have substantial forms of living beings. And these are the kinds of substantial forms that Aquinas calls *souls*. A soul, therefore, is simply *the substantial form of a living being*.[8]

8. "The soul . . . is the form of the living body"; "The soul gives not only substance and body (as a stone's form does) but life also." Thomas Aquinas, *Commentary on Aristotle's* De anima, trans. Kenelm Foster, OP and Sylvester Humphries, OP (New Haven: Yale University Press, 1951), 2.1.4.271 and 2.1.1.225.

Soul: first principle of vital activity

In the previous section, we saw that Aquinas characterizes the soul as the substantial form of a living being. This means that the soul is the principle of specification of a substance; that is, the soul *determines* the stuff that a living being is made out of to be a determinate *kind* or *species* of thing. Thus, Rover is a dog and acts as a dog because he is a dog. And he is a dog because he has the substantial form of a dog.

To be a dog, however, entails not just the fact of being a dog, but also having the *capabilities* for and the exercising of *activities* typical of a dog. Rover doesn't just sit on the floor and exist as a dog; he sniffs around, he wags his tail, he gobbles down pepperoni pizza.

We can say the same thing about ducks, and in fact, we know something is a duck because if it walks like a duck and quacks like a duck, it must be . . . a duck.

All of this leads us to consider the soul from another angle. If a duck is a duck because of the substantial form of a duck, and if the duck acts like a duck because it is a duck, then we should be able to say that the principle of the duck's *activity* as a duck is, ultimately, its form of a duck. In other words, the substantial form of duck not only determines a duck to be a duck, but it is also the primary principle of its acting as a duck. The soul is, in other words, the primary principle of the duck's vital operations.

If we expand this to all living beings, we can then say that the soul is *the primary principle of a living being's vital operations.*[9] As we shall see, Aquinas identifies and enumerates these vital

9. "The soul is that by which we primarily live, perceive, and think." Aristotle, *De anima* 2.2.414a13. For more on the soul as the substantial form of a living being and as its principle of activity from a Thomistic perspective, see Stephen L. Brock, *The Philosophy of Thomas Aquinas: A Sketch* (Eugene, OR: Wipf and Stock, 2015), pp. 53–57.

operations, and those will be the object of study of the next several chapters.

SUMMARY

Before moving on to the study of the various vital operations of living things, let us take a brief pause to review the main points we have discussed in this chapter.

1. Some physical beings are alive, though others are not.
2. Living beings are characterized by self-movement.
3. "Life" is primarily said of living beings and secondarily of the vital operations of these beings.
4. The principle of life in a living being is the soul.
5. The soul is the substantial form of a living being.
6. The soul is the first principle of a living being's vital operations.

CHAPTER 2

Organic Body

The Substantial Unity of Body and Soul

Aristotle and Aquinas' understanding of the soul as the substantial form of a living body implies that they do not conceive soul and body as two separate things that exist separate from or next to each other. For them, it is not as if the body existed by itself prior to its union with the soul. Nor did the soul exist as something previous to the body, just waiting for a body that it could enter into. Such dualistic conceptualizations of the relationship of body and soul are foreign to the Aristotelian and Thomistic way of thinking.[1]

Instead, what Aristotle and Aquinas propose is that when we are considering a living being, what exists is just that one individual living being. Now, as we have seen, this one individual being is composed of two principles: body and soul, which act as matter and substantial form of the living being. But, although body and soul are distinct *principles*, they are not distinct, separate things. Here, Aquinas offers the analogy of a wax figure: just as the wax figure is one thing, although its figure can be distinguished from the wax,

1. "We must not think, therefore, of the soul and body as though the body had its own form making it a body, to which a soul is superadded, making it a living body; but rather that the body gets both its being and its life from the soul." Aquinas, *Commentary on Aristotle's* De anima 2.1.1.225.

the living substance is one, although its substantial form (the soul) can be distinguished from the stuff or the matter that it informs (the body).

In the following paragraph, Msgr. Robert Sokolowski summarizes this understanding of living things and uses the word *animation* to describe the soul:

> Soul is proper to all material living things: men, animals, insects, and plants have soul, but soul is not something separate from their bodies. Soul is not a separate entity, not a ghost in a machine, and we must try to speak about it in such a way that we do not give the impression that it is a separate thing. A good synonym for the word *soul* is *animation*, and this word has an important advantage: we are much less tempted to think that the animation of a living thing could be found apart from that thing. You cannot have animation all by itself; it has to animate something. Animation or soul makes a living thing to be one thing, one entity. Soul is the unity of a living thing. It is also the source of the activities that thing carries out when it acts as a unified whole.[2]

The substantial unity of body and soul has important repercussions for understanding the organic body of a living being (the next section) and of the powers and operations of the soul (the following chapters).

---

2. Robert Sokolowski, "Soul and the Transcendence of the Human Person," in *Christian Faith and Human Understanding: Studies on the Eucharist, Trinity, and the Human Person* (Washington, DC: The Catholic University of America Press, 2006), p. 154.

The Organic Body

An instrumental (organic) body

The soul is the substantial form of a living being and, as such, it determines or makes that living being the *sort* of being that it is, with the *sort* of living body of that specific kind of being. Thus, Rover is a dog because he has the substantial form of a dog, and Rover has the sort of body that is that of a dog because of that same substantial form (or soul). For this reason, Aristotle describes the soul as "the actualization of a *certain sort* of body."[3] This is also why the "soul neither exists without a body nor is a body of some sort. For it is not a body, but belongs to a body, and for this reason, is present in a body, and in a body of such-and-such a sort."[4]

Now, if we look more closely at how Aristotle and Aquinas describe the sorts of bodies that are alive, we find that, aside from being natural bodies that are alive, they are described as bodies that are *organic* or *instrumental*.[5]

An organic (or instrumental) body is a body that has distinct parts, each of which has different physical characteristics and dispositions. It is through these organs that the soul exercises different vital operations.

Aquinas describes such an organic or instrumental body as "any body equipped with the various organs required by a living body in consequence of the life-principle's various vital activities. . . . For from this principle (the soul) which is the

3. Aristotle, *De anima* 2.2.414a17, emphasis added.

4. Aristotle, *De anima* 2.2.414a18–20.

5. "This sort of body would be one that is *instrumental*." Aristotle, *De anima* 2.1.412a27, emphasis added. The soul is "the first actualization of a *natural instrumental body*." Aristotle, *De anima* 2.1.412b5, emphasis added.

richest of embodied forms, spring many different activities, so that it requires, in the matter informed by it, a full equipment of different organs."[6]

A tree, for example, has roots through which it draws water and nutrients from the ground and leaves through which it can absorb light from the sun and transform it into energy that it needs to maintain itself. Another example is our eyes, which have different types of photoreceptive cells that make it possible for us to see in color.

Degrees of Life

Life shows itself in different ways

Living beings come in different forms. Wherever we look, we find various species of living beings, and we observe how they perform different types of activities.[7]

Aquinas, too, took notice of the diversity of living beings and operations. In a passage from his *Summa Theologiae*, he offers a basic overview of different types of living beings and their operations:

> Some living things have a nature capable only of *taking nourishment* and of what follows from this, viz., growth and generation; other living things have, in addition, a nature capable of *sensing*, as is clear in the case of immobile animals such as oysters; others also have, along with these operations, natures capable of *moving themselves by local movement*, e.g., perfect animals like quadrupeds and birds,

6. Aquinas, *Commentary on Aristotle's* De anima 2.1.1.230.

7. "Things are said to be living in many ways." Aristotle, *De anima* 2.2.413a21–22.

> etc.; and still others have, in addition, a nature capable of *understanding*, e.g., men.[8]

In his commentary on Aristotle's *De anima*, Aquinas goes further and classifies different degrees or modes of life:

> There are (four such) degrees, distinguished in the same way as the four modes in which life is manifested: for some living things, i.e., plants, only take nourishment and grow and decay; some have also sensation, but are always fixed to one place—such are the inferior animals like shell-fish; some again, i.e. the complete animals like oxen and horses, have, along with sensation, the power to move from place to place; and finally some, i.e. men, have, in addition, mind.[9]

From this, Aquinas identifies three different souls: vegetative souls (of plants), sentient souls (of inferior and complete animals), and rational souls (of animals that have reason). These souls are, moreover, related to each other hierarchically, from the most basic (vegetative souls) to the higher and more complex (sentient and rational souls) ones:

> Aristotle likens the nature of things to numbers; which increase by tiny degrees, one by one. Thus among living things there are some, i.e. plants, which have only the vegetative capacity—which, indeed, they must have because no living being could maintain an existence in matter without the vegetative activities. Next are the animals, with sensitivity as well as vegetative life; and sensitivity implies a third power, appetition, which itself divides into three: into desire, in the stricter sense, which springs from the concupiscible appetite;

---

8. Aquinas, *Summa Theologiae* 1.18.2.

9. Aquinas, *Commentary on Aristotle's* De anima, 2.1.3.255.

> anger, corresponding to the irascible appetite—both of these being in the sensitive part and following sense-knowledge; and finally will, which is the intellectual appetite and follows intellectual apprehension.[10]

We will consider these various types of souls, along with their powers and operations, in the sections and chapters that follow. But first we must take a closer look at an aspect of living things; namely, their powers and operations.

Powers and Operations

Life, as we have seen, involves self-movement: it involves a variety of vital activities, or, to use more technical language, vital *operations*. These include, but are not limited to, nutrition, growth, sense knowing, feelings, thinking, and free choice.

As we will examine in more detail in the chapters that follow, each type of vital operation involves some particular aspect of the material world that the operation focuses on, and it is this that Aquinas calls the *object* of that operation. Thus, for example, we say that the object of the operation of seeing is color, while the object of hearing is sound. We will consider the various operations and their objects later, but at this point, what we want to have clear is (a) vital activities are called vital *operations*; and (b) each kind of vital operation has a proper *object*, which is that aspect of material reality that the specific operation deals with.

As we have been seeing, a living being's life manifests itself in (and in some way consists of) a number of vital operations.

---

10. Aquinas, *Commentary on Aristotle's* De anima 2.3.5.288. Also: "The parts of the soul follow each other in a series like the kinds of geometrical figure. . . . The parts of soul follow one from the other successively. The sensitive part . . . cannot exist without the vegetative, but the latter can, in plants, exist without the sensitive." Aquinas, *Commentary on Aristotle's* De anima 2.3.6.300.

Rover, for example, when presented with a slice of pizza, senses it, hungers for it, eats it, savors it, and digests it. All these are vital operations of a dog. A dog, however, is not always looking at pizza, hungering for pizza, or digesting pizza. Even when it is not performing these activities, the dog continues to have the capacities or, to use Aquinas' vocabulary, the "powers" or "faculties" to exercise these operations. Expanding from this particular example, we can understand that all living beings have a set of capabilities or powers to exercise specific operations. In Aristotle and Aquinas' view, then, we have three interlocking pieces that structure and explain a living being's activity: (a) *powers or faculties*, which are capacities to execute vital operations; (b) the vital *operations* themselves; and (c) the *proper objects* of each operation, which are those aspects of material reality that a particular operation deals with.

This way of understanding powers, operations, and objects enables Aquinas to clearly identify, enumerate, and examine the various vital operations in living things, and to do so in an orderly, structured way. At this point, though, we should recall how Aquinas identifies different types of souls—more specifically, vegetative souls, sentient souls, and rational souls. Each of these is characterized by specific vital operations and thus entails different powers. At the same time, as we saw earlier in this chapter, Aquinas affirms that the soul exercises these operations through different organic parts of the body. It is these powers and operations (and their objects) that we will now study.

The Vegetative Soul and Its Powers

The basic form of life is what Aquinas calls vegetative life, and this is the kind of life lived by the most basic of living beings—namely, plants. Vegetative life involves three vital operations: two ordered to maintaining the life of the individual living being (nourishment and growth), and one ordered to the conservation of the species (reproduction). These three vital operations entail three different powers of the vegetative soul.[11]

The nutritive power

The nutritive power is the capacity to take food so that the living being might maintain itself.[12] Through the exercise of this power, the living being ingests food from which it extracts the nutrients and absorbs the energy that it needs to maintain itself in being. The organism does this through organs of the body that, in animals, form the digestive system. In human beings, this system consists of the gastrointestinal tract (which includes the mouth, esophagus, stomach, and large and small intestines), along with the accessory organs of digestion (the tongue, salivary glands, pancreas, liver, and gallbladder).

The augmentative power

The augmentative power is ordered to the operation of growth "through which the living body acquires its appropriate size."[13] This growth includes not only an increase in bulk but also differentiated growth by which a living organism's

---

11. "Among lower things life is received in a corruptible nature that requires generation for the conservation of the species and nourishment for the conservation of the individual." Aquinas, *Summa Theologiae* 1.18.3.

12. "The nutritive power . . . is simply that faculty by which a living being is able to maintain itself as such; while food is the condition of this faculty's activity, that by means of which it maintains its subject." Aquinas, *Commentary on Aristotle's* De anima 2.4.9.345.

13. Aquinas, *Summa Theologiae* 1.78.2.

body develops the organs it needs to peform vital operations. A plant, for example, begins as a seed, develops into a sprout, then a seedling (now with roots and leaves), and then into a budding and flowering plant (with buds, flowers, and fruit). In animals, this process of growth is even more elaborate, as can be seen in the process of embryogenesis, which begins with the fertilization of an egg cell and continues as the living creature develops into a zygote and embryo. As it grows and develops, structures and organic systems form and develop. This process of growth continues even after birth and, in the case of human beings, continues for many years into young adulthood.

The generative power

The generative power is ordered toward an operation through which an individual of a species comes to be (and this is further ordered to the conservation of the species).[14] In nature, we find a great variety of ways living beings reproduce: from simple division of one-celled living beings to plant reproduction involving pollination, fruit, and seeds to the various kinds of sexual reproduction in animals.

SUMMARY

1. The body and the soul of a living being form one substantial unity.
2. The body of a living being is an organic body, meaning that it has differentiated parts called organs through which the soul exercises different vital operations.

14. See Aquinas, *Summa Theologiae* 1.78.2.

3. A power or faculty of the soul is the capability to exercise specific vital operations.
4. There are different kinds of souls: vegetative souls, sentient souls, and rational souls.
5. The vegetative soul has three powers (and operations): the nutritive power, the augmentative power, and the generative power.
6. These powers are ordered to operations that maintain both the life of the individual living being and the continuation of the species.

CHAPTER 3

Sense Knowledge

Sentient Life

Methuselah, a bristlecone pine tree at the Ancient Bristlecone Pine Forest in the White Mountains in Inyo County in eastern California, is, at 4,855 years old, the oldest known living individual tree in the world. To prevent tourists from damaging its fragile root system, the US Forest Service refuses to say exactly where it is. Like other plants, Methuselah has a soul (in this case, a vegetative soul), and for 4,855 years this soul has been the principle of its vital operations, operations that are typical of a bristlecone pine tree. For 4,855 years, Methuselah has been converting energy from the sun and drawing nutrients from the ground to keep itself alive. We will assume that Methuselah continues to grow and that it may still be able to reproduce. But where has Methuselah been all these years? If tourists do find it, will Methuselah uproot itself and sneak away? Although Methuselah has outlived almost every other living creature in its neighborhood, we assume that it has, for 4,855 years, always been where it is now.

Meanwhile, other living things, such as bighorn sheep, mule deer, marmots, and feral horses, roam the surrounding area of the White Mountains. These living beings do not root themselves in one place, and their lives are not limited to the basic vegetative operations of plants. While they too eat, grow, and reproduce, their lives actively involve much more. They sense other beings that are at a distance from them, they are capable of responding to what they sense with feelings and inclinations, and they are able to move from one place to another.

Aquinas calls these kinds of living beings *sentient beings* or *animals*, and this is now where we focus our attention.

For Aquinas, there are different types of animals of varying complexity and perfection, ranging from immovable animals that only have the basic sense of touch to those that sense and react to beings around themselves and are capable of moving from one place to another. Broadly speaking, Aquinas identifies three types of powers that are typical of the sentient soul (the soul of animals):

1. *Sense-knowing powers*, by which the animal is able to know things that are outside of itself and to evaluate whether they are suitable or harmful to itself
2. *Sense-appetitive powers*, by which the animal can respond to what it senses in the form of feelings or passions (inclinations toward or away from what it senses)
3. *Locomotive powers*, by which the animal can move from place to place

In this chapter, we will consider the powers and sense operations by which an animal is able to know beings outside itself (the external and the internal sense powers). In the next chapter, we will examine the powers and operations by which the animal tends toward or away from the beings that it senses (the sense appetites and their passions).

The External Sense Powers

For Aristotle and Aquinas, all knowledge of external things comes to us first through our external senses. In nature, substances have qualities that we can sense. We sense these qualities through our *external sense powers*, which are *powers or capabilities to sense these sensible qualities that are in things*. Each external sense power exercises its operation through a part of the organism's being that acts as the physical organ of that power.[1]

The power of sight, for example, requires a physical organ capable of receiving color (or, from a more modern understanding, electromagnetic waves within a certain range of frequencies), and we find that the eye, with its photoreceptive cells, has just the right receptiveness to light that is needed for us to see. The same can be said of the powers and organs of hearing, smelling, tasting, and touch.

Aquinas identifies five external sense powers. While it is possible, in the light of modern biology, to argue that there are fewer or more of these sense powers, these five are those that have been accepted for centuries and are still a point of reference today.

Here we should recall something mentioned in the previous chapter. For Aquinas, a power is a capability to exercises certain operations. At the same time, each operation involves an aspect of reality, which is called its *object*. Thus, in the enumeration below, we will mention (a) the power, (b) the operation, and (c) the object. To make it easier, we will indicate the power with bold font, the operation with italics, and the object by using capital letters. For example the **power of sight** (=the **power**) *sees* (=the *operation*) COLOR (=OBJECT).

1. "Nothing has sensation without a body, since the action of sensing cannot proceed from the soul except through a corporeal organ." Aquinas, *Summa Theologiae* 1.77.5.

The five external sense powers (with their operations and objects) are the following:

The **power of sight** *sees* COLOR.

The **power of hearing** *hears* SOUNDS.

The **power of smell** *smells* ODORS.

The **power of taste** *tastes* FLAVORS.

The **power of touch** *feels or senses* a number of qualities such as HOT OR COLD, WET OR DRY.

Sensible Cognition

How does sense cognition work?

In the previous section, we considered what external sense powers are, and what their operations and objects are. But just how does sense cognition work?

According to Aquinas, knowledge begins when a sensible quality in something outside the animal physically alters the sense organ of one of the animal's external sense powers. This alteration then makes it possible for the sense power to pass from *potentially* sensing that quality to *actually* sensing it. And it is this actually sensing a sensible quality that is the vital operation of the sense power.

Since this is quite a bit to take in all at once, let us look at this process more slowly.

On the one hand, we have an animal with an external sense power (a capability to sense some specific sensible quality).

On the other hand, we have an external material substance that has qualities that can be sensed (sensible qualities).

To illustrate, let us take Rover as our animal. As a dog, Rover has a number of capabilities or *powers*. One of them is the external sense *power of smell*. As a power, it is capable of exercising a *vital operation*. In this particular case, the power of smell is the capability to exercise the vital operation of *smelling*. Now, as with all vital operations, smelling is concerned with some specific aspect of reality, which is called is proper *object*. Here, the proper object of smelling is an *odor*.

As an example of a material substance outside of Rover, let us take pepperoni pizza (with a touch of crushed red pepper flakes and jalapeño slices). Pepperoni pizza has several qualities that are sensible: color, odor, and taste, for example. Here, we are interested in the sensible quality of the pizza that is the proper object of Rover's power of smell, which is the odor or aroma of pepperoni pizza.

Now, how does Rover come to sense or smell the odor of pepperoni pizza?

As we said, sense knowledge begins with an alteration of a sense organ by a sensible quality. In our example, the pizza has qualities that can affect or alter the sense organ of a dog's power of smelling. Exactly how this happens is quite complex, but it involves a number of aromatic molecules that pass through the air until they arrive at Rover's olfactory organs (his nose, olfactory bulb, and so on). Rover's olfactory organs are parts of his dog body that is disposed in such a way that they serve as the physical organ and part of Rover's power to smell. In order for Rover to pass from potentially smelling pepperoni pizza to actually smelling it, the physical sense organ of his power of smell (which is mainly his nose) needs to somehow be altered by the sense qualities of the pizza. This happens when the complex aromatic molecules arrive from the pizza to Rover's nose. There, various chemical receptors in his olfactory bulb receive these molecules, which in turn activate a series of nerve signals that are transmitted to Rover's brain.

All this forms part of the physical conditions required for Rover to actually smell the pizza. If Rover's olfactory organs are correctly stimulated, his power of smell passes from potentially smelling pepperoni pizza to actually smelling it. And it is at this point that Rover has the *sensation* of smelling his favorite type of pizza.

Looking back, we can identify two basic steps that result in an animal's actually sensing material beings.

> Step 1: the sensible quality of a material substance modifies (alters) the physical sense organ of an external sense power.
>
> Step 2: this actualizes the sense power so that it passes from potentially sensing its proper sense object to actually sensing that object.

Neuroscience and sensation

The difference between steps 1 and 2 is important for many reasons, one of which is that it distinguishes the physiological process that sensation requires from the actual sensation experienced by the animal. Step 1 involves physiological and physicochemical processes that can be empirically measured and observed. Step 2 involves the actual sensation that the animal experiences, a psychic phenomenon of the soul that is not completely reducible to the physical activity observable in Step 1. In other words, the physicochemical processes needed for Rover to smell the pizza are not exactly the same as Rover's actual sensation of smelling that pizza.

What we can say is that from a Thomistic perspective, the physical alteration of the sense organ, along with the physiological changes that accompany it, do not, in themselves, constitute the sense knowing itself, but rather form physical precursors that are necessary for that sensation. The actual sensation (or sense knowing) is an operation of the sense power, which does not completely coincide with the physical changes that occur in the sense organ.

For this reason, while neuroscience can explain the mechanisms and physiology of the physical sense organ, it does not deal directly with the sensation itself, nor with the nature of the sense power as such.

Thus, the scientist investigates the physiological events that touching a hot boiled egg entails (including increased skin temperature, firing of nerve cells, action of neurotransmitters, and so on), while the philosopher asks about the reality of the vital operation that is experienced as a sensation or a feeling of that egg's hotness, and of the nature of the principles through which I have those sensations (the powers of the soul and the soul itself).

The Internal Sense Powers

What is an internal sense power?

While animals are capable of sensing qualities of things outside themselves, their perception of the individual substances around them is much more than a kaleidoscope of disjointed sensations: a color here, a sound there, an odor over there. Another interesting dimension of animal behavior is that their engagement with the things they sense is not limited to the moments when physical stimuli are received. Instead, they are capable of determining their behavior toward a thing even when that thing is no longer immediately present to their senses. That is, animals not only perceive things that are immediately present to it; they must be able in some way to *retain* and *conserve* the qualities that they once received and perceived. This entails that in addition to external senses (by which animals receive and perceive sensible qualities in the present), they also need to have powers by which they *retain* and *conserve* those sense impressions.[2] These powers are what Aquinas calls the *internal senses*.

Aquinas identifies four internal senses: (1) the common sense; (2) the imagination; (3) the estimative power; and (4) the memory.

Each of these powers has its own operation, and each operation has its own object. Also, like the external sense powers, the internal senses require a physical organ that they use as an instrument through which they exercise their specific operations. Exactly which organs of the body correspond to which internal sense is not always clear in Aquinas, but today a good case could be made for identifying the organs of the internal senses with various parts of the nervous system, especially the brain.

The common sense

Animals perceive sensible qualities in things through the exercise of their external sense powers. Classically, there are five external sense powers, each with its own operation and proper object: seeing sees color; hearing hears sounds; smell smells odors; taste tastes flavors; touch feels hot or cold, wet or dry. Each external sense power senses its own proper object, and a number of consequences follow from this.

First, any particular external sense power senses its own proper object, but does not sense the proper object of a

---

2. "Therefore, through its sentient soul the animal must not only receive the species of sensible things when it is presently being affected by those things, but must also retain and conserve the species." Aquinas, *Summa Theologiae* 1.78.4.

different sense power. For example, the power of sight sees color, but it does not see odors. As a consequence, no one external sense power can distinguish the proper object of one sense power from the proper object of another sense power. That is, for example, no external sense power can distinguish white from sweet.

Second, an external sense power senses its proper object, but does not sense its own sensing. For example, the power of sight sees color, but does not see its own seeing.

Questions thus arise: How does the animal distinguish between the various proper objects of the different external senses? How does the animal know that it is sensing?

This is where what Aquinas called *the common sense* comes in. The common sense (not to be confused with "common sense" as we use the phrase in ordinary language when we want to say that something should be evident and needs no explanation) is an internal sense power. Its primary functions are (a) to serve as a common terminus to which all the apprehensions of the senses are referred; and (b) to perceive when an external sense power is actually operating.[3]

For example, Rover smells the odor of the pepperoni pizza with his power of smell and sees the color of the pizza with his

---

3. "Neither the sense of sight nor the sense of taste can distinguish white from sweet, since whatever makes a distinction between two things must have cognition of both of them. Hence, the judgment regarding this distinction must belong to the common sensory power, which is such that (a) all the apprehensions of the senses are referred to it as to a common terminus, and such that (b) it also perceives the intentions of the sensory powers, as when someone sees that he is seeing. For the latter cannot be done through a proper sensory power, which has cognition only of the sensible form by which it is changed. The act of seeing is perfected in such a change, and from this change there follows another change in the common sensory power, which perceives the act of seeing." Aquinas, *Summa Theologiae* 1.78.4.

power of sight. Now, with his common sense, Rover is able to do two things: (a) his smelling the odor of the pizza and his seeing the color of it come together and can be distinguished from each other; and (b) he can tell that he is smelling and seeing (although we should add that he is not self-aware of doing so).

The imagination

For an animal to successfully interact with material beings, it needs to be able to act not just on the immediate stimuli it receives from these things, but also when their perception is absent or incomplete. For this, the animal needs to (a) somehow retain these sense impressions and (b) re-elaborate them even when the original sense stimuli are no longer present. This is the role of the internal sense that Aquinas calls the *imagination*.[4]

An important function of the imagination is that it forms an image (also called a phantasm), which is basically a unified perception of the individual thing that the animal is sensing. Thus, it is with his imagination that Rover forms a unified perception of the individual pepperoni pizza (it color, its odor, its shape, and other sensible aspects of the pizza). And this is true both when the pizza is sitting in front of him and when I try to hide it from him by walking into another room or placing it under the table.

For rational animals (which we will study in chapter 5), the phantasm formed by the imagination plays an important role insofar as it is from this phantasm or image that the intellect abstracts the essence (the quiddity or *what*) of the thing.

---

4. "The *imaging power* or *power of imagining* (*phantasia vel imaginatio*)—they are the same—is ordered toward the retention or conservation of forms. For the imaging (or imagining) power is, as it were, a sort of treasury of forms that have been received through the sensory power." Aquinas, *Summa Theologiae* 1.78.4.

Human beings, unlike other animals, are also able to creatively combine images into what we often call "works of the imagination."

The estimative power

A fascinating dimension of animal behavior is that they not only perceive things, but they also seem to be able to evaluate what they perceive as being either suitable or harmful to them. But how does this occur? It is certainly not because there are colors or odors that are intrinsically dangerous or advantageous to the organism that perceives them. Here, Aquinas once again concludes that there must be an internal sense power by which the animal is able to determine whether something is suitable or harmful to it. Aquinas calls this the *estimative power*.

Aquinas illustrates this with two examples. First, when a sheep sees a wolf, it flees "not because of the ugliness of the wolf's color or shape, but because of the danger to the sheep's nature." The second is when a bird collects straw "not because the straw delights its senses, but because this is useful for building a nest."[5]

If we look back to Rover, we see that Rover is not only able to perceive the pizza but is able to evaluate it as something "suitable" to him.

In human beings, this power to evaluate the suitability of something perceived is called the *cogitative power*, since it is connected with the power of reason. For Aquinas, nonrational animals are able to evaluate the suitability of things they sense by a sort of natural instinct, whereas rational animals make these evaluations "through a certain comparison."[6]

---

5. Aquinas, *Summa Theologiae* 1.78.4.

6. Aquinas, *Summa Theologiae* 1.78.4.

The memory

Finally, there is the power that retains the evaluations made by the estimative power. Aquinas calls this the *memory*. Through the operation of the memory, an animal not only evaluates based on inborn instinct but is also able to retain and remember what has, in fact, been harmful or beneficial to it, and thus is able to learn and adjust its evaluations of suitability through experience.

To consider Rover once again, we can say that Rover can learn, as he gains experience in pizza eating, which types of pizza would turn out to be more "suitable" for him.

SUMMARY

1. The sentient soul has, in addition to the powers of the vegetative soul, cognitive sense powers, sense appetites, and locomotive power.
2. As with all powers of the soul, each power is a capacity to exercise operations and each operation has an object.
3. The cognitive sense powers are divided into external sense powers and internal sense powers.
4. The five external senses are: sight, hearing, smell, taste, touch.
5. The internal senses (which continue sensible knowledge) are: the common sense, the imagination, the estimative power (cogitative in rational beings), and the memory.

CHAPTER 4

Sense Appetites and Passions

Feelings

Do animals experience feelings? If so, what feelings do they feel? And how can we tell? When a dog growls, is it angry? When a deer sees you and flees, is it experiencing fear? When Rover wags his tail as you place a piece of pepperoni pizza in front of him, is he feeling desire?

Close observation of animals seems to indicate that they do, in fact, have feelings. Animals such as horses, pigs, rats, and cats move their bodies in ways that seem to express feelings. The way their ears change position or the amount of eyewhite they display can indicate pain or fear in animals.[1] Vocalizations such as grunts, bleats, moos, and barks are also interpreted as expressions of emotions felt by animals. More recent scientific studies focus on measuring changes in the autonomic nervous system (heart rate, blood pressure, respiration) or hormone concentrations as ways of determining if an animal is experiencing emotion.

1. For an attempt at using machine language to link mouse facial expressions with basic feelings such as joy, fear, and pain, see Nate Dolensek et al., "Facial Expressions of Emotion States and Their Neuronal Correlates in Mice," *Science* 368, no. 6486 (April 3, 2020), pp. 89–94, https://www.science.org/doi/10.1126/science.aaz9468.

Aristotle and Aquinas took as evident that animals not only know individual material beings through their senses, but also that this knowledge is often accompanied by the experience of feelings for these things. Thus, they concluded, feelings are vital operations that form part of the life of sentient beings as they interact with the world that surrounds them. This chapter focuses on Aquinas' understanding of the powers and operations by which animals affectively engage with the reality that they capture with their sense.

Sense Appetites and Their Passions

The sensible appetite

Aside from knowing things with external and internal senses, an animal's life also involves the capability to tend toward or away from things that it evaluates as being suitable or harmful to it. This activity of tending toward or away from something sensed is what we commonly call *feelings*, or, in Thomas Aquinas' philosophical language, *passions*. The capability or power to feel or to have a passion is called a *sensible appetite*.

In chapter 3, we saw how an external (or internal) sense power is the capability of exercising certain actions or operations by which the animal knows an individual material substance or one of its qualities (for example, the power of sight is the capability of seeing color). A sense appetite is a power too, but instead of being a capability to know or sense a material substance, it is a capacity to *feel* or to have a *passion* about what is apprehended. Both sense powers and sense appetites are powers, but they differ in the kinds of operations they carry out and in the objects of those operations. Sense powers "know" their objects, while sense appetites are "moved" by or "tend" toward or away from (that is, they have feelings or passions with regard to) their objects.[2]

The estimative power and the sensible appetites

Although the external and internal sense powers are distinct from the sensible appetite, they are nevertheless related to one another. The process by which passions arise in the sensible appetite does not, in fact, begin with the appetite itself, but with the operation of the estimative power, which is one of the internal sense powers. It will be recalled that it is the estimative power that evaluates the suitability or harmfulness of an individual substance that the animal comes to know through its senses. This evaluation is then passed on to and activates the sensible appetite in such a way that the animal experiences feelings or passions with regard to what it has apprehended through the senses. The concrete passion that is activated depends on a number of factors, including whether what the animal has sensed has been evaluated as suitable (agreeable) or harmful (disagreeable) and whether what is perceived is immediately present or is instead difficult to obtain or to avoid.

For example, when we place a piece of pepperoni pizza in front of Rover, he not only knows its qualities with his external senses and forms an image of pizza in his imagination; his estimate power also evaluates the pizza as "good," that is, as suitable to him. This evaluation of the pizza is presented to his sense appetite, which is then activated as a feeling or passion with regard to the pizza (in this case, the feeling of love and desire for the pizza).

---

2. See Aquinas, *Summa Theologiae* 1-2.23.2–3.

Linguistic considerations

As Aquinas enumerates and classifies the various feelings that an animal can experience, he divides the sensible appetite into two: the *concupiscible appetite*, which has to do with things that are immediately attainable or avoidable; and the *irascible appetite*, which involves things that are difficult to obtain or to avoid.[3]

Aquinas identifies six passions of the concupiscible appetite and five of the irascible appetite.

But before we enumerate and name these passions, we need to consider a linguistic difficulty that arises when we use words to describe feelings. As we have been seeing, passions (or feelings) are activities of the sensible appetite that arise when the animal senses an external material substance and evaluates it as being either suitable or harmful to it. During our presentation of the passions, we should thus keep in mind that, although the passions are activities of the sensible soul, they are not, in themselves, rational activities. This means that their reality is expressed not so much with rational concepts and words, but with prerational or infra-rational vocalizations, facial expressions, and other corporeal movements.

It is for this reason that our presentation of the passions will begin with emotive descriptions (the prerational bodily

3. "Therefore, since the sentient appetite is an inclination that follows upon sentient apprehension . . . it must be the case that in the sentient part of the soul there are two appetitive powers: (a) one through which the soul is simply inclined to pursue those things that are agreeable according to the senses and to avoid those things that are harmful, and this is called the *concupiscible* power; and (b) a second through which the animal resists aggressors that pose obstacles to what is agreeable and that inflict harm, and this is called the *irascible* power. Hence, the object of the irascible power is said to be what is difficult (*arduum*), because the irascible power tends toward overcoming contraries and winning out over them." Aquinas, *Summa Theologiae* 1.81.2.

expressions or vocalizations that accompany different feelings) before giving the word that Aquinas uses to designate that specific passion.

The intention behind this is to invite the reader first to imagine the feeling being presented before attempting to conceptualize it and give it a name.

The concupiscible appetite and its passions

The concupiscible appetitive power is that power by which the soul is "simply inclined to pursue those things that are agreeable to the senses and to avoid those things that are harmful."[4] If what is sensed has been evaluated as suitable or agreeable to the organism and if it is immediately accessible, then three passions of the concupiscible appetite arise.

We can illustrate this by returning to Rover and describing what he feels when he senses pepperoni pizza.

First, there is a feeling of "oh!" as Rover's eyes widen and he begins to wag his tail. This awakening of the appetite that takes the form of an initial attraction to something is what Aquinas calls *love* (*amor* in Latin).[5] This is akin to what we mean when we say, "I *love* chocolate ice cream!" This love is basically a physiological love, and is obviously different from the personal and spiritual love between persons, which is an act of the will. (We will examine this later, in chapter 6.)

The second passion that Rover experiences is when he begins to move toward the pizza with the intention of taking possession of it. This is the feeling of "mmm" that Rover feels as he is drawn and moves toward the pizza. Aquinas calls this

4. Aquinas, *Summa Theologiae* 1.81.2.

5. See Aquinas, *Summa Theologiae* 1-2.26–28.

passion (for something that one is moving toward but does not yet possess) *desire* (Latin: *desiderium* or *concupiscentia*).[6]

Finally, when Rover gets the pizza, another passion arises: a feeling of satisfaction expressed as "mmMMM!" Aquinas calls this *pleasure* or *joy* (Latin: *delectatio*, *gaudium*, or *laetitia*).[7]

We thus have three passions that come with the apprehension of something suitable or agreeable (also called a "sensible good"): (1) *love*, when the sensible good is first presented to the animal; (2) *desire*, when the animal is moving to obtain that reality; and (3) *joy*, when the animal comes to possess that sensible good.

Three different passions arise when the animal is presented with something that is considered harmful or disagreeable.

Dogs, for some reason, find citrus repulsive (at least according to thewildest.com). So, if we attempt to push an orange slice toward Rover, he first reacts with an "ew" feeling. Aquinas calls this *hatred* (Latin: *odium*).[8]

If we insist and continue to push the orange slice toward Rover, he begins to pull back. Aquinas calls this "nooooo" feeling *aversion* (Latin: *fuga* or *abominatio*).

And finally, if we successfully force the orange slice into Rover's mouth, we get the "yuck!" feeling, which Aquinas calls *pain* or *sadness* (Latin: *dolor* or *tristitia*).[9]

Thus, here too, three passions arise with the apprehension of something immediately harmful or disagreeable (or, more technically, a "sensible evil"): (1) *hatred*, when the animal is first presented with something harmful or disagreeable; (2) *aversion*,

6. See Aquinas, *Summa Theologiae* 1-2.30.

7. See Aquinas, *Summa Theologiae* 1-2.31–34.

8. See Aquinas, *Summa Theologiae* 1-2.29.

9. See Aquinas, *Summa Theologiae* 1-2.35–39.

as the animal strives to move away or avoid something deemed harmful; and (3) *sadness* or *pain*, when the animal is forced to endure something harmful.

The six passions covered so far (love, desire, joy, hatred, aversion, and sadness) are concerned with things that are either suitable or harmful, as well as being immediately accessible or present. They are considered the passions of the concupiscible sense appetite.

The irascible appetite and its passions

The irascible appetitive power is the power through which the animal resists aggressors that pose obstacles to what is agreeable and inflict harm. Its object is "what is difficult," and its passions tend toward overcoming difficulties and obstacles and winning over them.[10]

Aquinas identifies five passions of the irascible appetite.

If the animal is presented with something suitable or desirable but difficult to obtain (thus called an *arduous* or *difficult sensible good*), then two possible passions arise.

To illustrate this, let us go back to Rover and the pepperoni pizza. But let us now make it difficult for Rover to get to the pizza, perhaps by putting it in a dish that we place up on a tree branch that is difficult to access. Here, the pizza, while still desirable, is no longer an easily accessible sensible good, but rather what Aquinas calls an arduous sensible good, one that is difficult to obtain and, as such, is the object of the irascible sense appetite.

If Rover clambers up the tree and, by some combination of skill and good luck, gets to a point where it seems that he just might be able to obtain this difficult piece of pizza, he becomes excited at

10. See Aquinas, *Summa Theologiae* 1.81.2.

the prospect. It is this feeling that Aquinas calls *hope* (Latin: *spes*).[11] This hope is, of course, distinct from the theological virtue of hope. Here, we are talking more about the *feeling* of hope that we feel when we find ourselves in a situation in which we realize that we might be able to achieve something important but difficult to obtain. Here, the example of sports might be of help: after a long and hard-fought football game, we feel hope if we are just a couple of yards away from a game-winning touchdown.

A different feeling arises if it seems that we might not, after all, achieve that goal. If Rover, for example, clambers up the tree but starts to falter and slip, there comes a moment when he realizes that the pizza might actually be beyond his grasp, and a feeling of discouragement arises. This is what Aquinas calls *despair* (Latin: *desperatio*).[12] In our football example, it's the feeling you experience when your team is one yard away from a touchdown but fails to get over the goal line on fourth down as time expires.

A different pair of passions arises when the animal encounters something undesirable and difficult to get rid of (an *arduous or difficult sensible evil*).

Here, we have to bring Rover in again. But this time, he is presented with a huge threat. For example, a velociraptor (recently escaped from Jurassic Park) threatens the life of the Rover's owner. When Rover first encounters the velociraptor, his estimative power evaluates it as (very) harmful and as (extremely) difficult to get rid of. Rover, nevertheless, attempts to defend his owner by entering into combat with the dinosaur.

If, at some point, after a series of exceptionally accurate lunges and flying kicks, Rover is able to stun the velociraptor, he begins to feel that he might actually be able to defeat

11. See Aquinas, *Summa Theologiae* 1-2.40.

12. See Aquinas, *Summa Theologiae* 1-2.40.4.

this evil. This feeling is what Aquinas calls *daring* or *courage* (Latin: *audacia*).[13] It's the same feeling expressed in *Rocky* movies, when Rocky senses that, against all odds, he might be able to defeat an imposing opponent (as the music changes to the iconic *Rocky* theme).

If, on the other hand, it is Rover who suffers an injury and is stunned, then the feeling of dread that comes with the realization that he might lose and succumb to the velociraptor arises. This unpleasant, panicky feeling is what Aquinas calls *fear* (Latin: *timor*).[14]

Finally, there is the situation in which the animal is faced with some sort of persistent unpleasantness being imposed upon it. For example, if you keep squirting orange juice into Rover's face, he will eventually explode with fury and try to bite you in order to get back at you. Aquinas calls this aggressive passion *anger* (Latin: *ira*).[15]

There are, then, five passions of the irascible appetite: (1) *hope*, when some arduous sensible good seems attainable; (2) *despair*, when some arduous sensible good seems to be no longer attainable; (3) *daring*, when it seems possible to overcome some difficult evil; (4) *fear*, when it seems that one might succumb to some difficult evil; and (5) *anger*, when faced with some injury that requires vengeance.

The Sensible Passions in Human Beings

Human beings, just like other animals, share in the life of sensible passions and feelings. Thus, on a basic level, our feelings

13. See Aquinas, *Summa Theologiae* 1-2.45.

14. See Aquinas, *Summa Theologiae* 1-2.41–44.

15. See Aquinas, *Summa Theologiae* 1-2.46–48.

arise from purely sensible causes: we perceive things with our senses, evaluate them on a sensible level as suitable or harmful, and respond accordingly with our passions and feelings.

At the same time, human beings have a higher dimension and are moved by the higher faculties of reason and will. Thus, in human beings, the sensible powers (the senses and the sensible appetites) are part of a broader set of powers that includes the rational powers of reason and will toward which they should be ordered and harmonized.[16]

But to understand how this works on a practical level, first we need to study the rational powers of the souls, namely the intellect (chapter 5) and the will (chapter 6), and then how the sensible appetites and their passions are perfected by being habitually ordered to act in accordance with reason (chapter 7).

SUMMARY

1. Animals not only know things outside of themselves, they also respond and are drawn or repulsed by them.
2. The vital activity of being attracted to or repulsed by something is called a feeling or passion.
3. The power to have feelings or passions is called a sense appetite.
4. The sense appetite is divided into the concupiscible appetite and the irascible appetite.
5. The concupiscible appetite has as its object something that is immediately agreeable or disagreeable (an immediate sensible good or an immediate sensible evil).

16. See Aquinas, *Summa Theologiae* 1.81.3.

6. The passions of the concupiscible appetite are love, desire, joy, hate, aversion, and pain.
7. The irascible appetite has as its object something suitable but difficult to obtain (an arduous sensible good) or something harmful but difficult to overcome (an arduous sensible evil).
8. The passions of the irascible appetite are hope, despair, daring, fear, and anger.
9. In human beings, the passions of the sensible appetite should be ordered to the exercise of the higher, rational powers (intellect and will).

CHAPTER 5

Intellect

An Animal That Has *Logos*

In his dialogue *Protagoras*, Plato relates an ancient Greek myth that explains how the gods, after molding mortal beings inside the earth, put Prometheus and Epimetheus in charge of distributing and assigning powers and abilities to each one. Plato continues the story:

> But Epimetheus was not very wise, and he absentmindedly used up all the powers and abilities on the nonreasoning animals; he was left with the human race, completely unequipped. While he was floundering about at a loss, Prometheus arrived to inspect the distribution and saw that while the other animals were well provided with everything, the human race was naked, unshod, unbedded, and unarmed, and it was already the day on which all of them, human beings included, were destined to emerge from the earth into the light. It was then that Prometheus, desperate to find some means of survival for the human race, stole from Hephaestus and Athena wisdom in the practical arts together with fire (without which this kind of wisdom is effectively useless) and gave them outright to the human race.[1]

1. Plato, *Protagoras*, trans. Stanley Lombardo and Karen Bell, in *Plato: Complete Works*, ed. John M. Cooper (Indianapolis: Hackett, 1997), 321b–d.

This story highlights two characteristics that distinguish human beings from other animals. First, they seem to lack the natural powers and abilities they need to survive. Second, this apparent deficiency is made up for by a gift that other animals do not have—namely, wisdom in the practical arts.

We find similar considerations in various Greek thinkers. Aristotle, for example, identifies reason (*logos*) as what distinguishes human beings from other animals.

Aquinas, for his part, takes as something given that what distinguishes human beings from other animals is that they exercise rational thought; that is, they perform operations of a sort that is clearly distinct and of another level from those performed by nonrational animals. These operations and the power to exercise them are so distinct that Aquinas considers them a completely different and higher degree of life.

In this chapter, we will examine the intellect and its operations, and then, in the following chapter (chapter 6), we will study the will, which is the appetite that follows upon the apprehension of the good by the intellect.

Sense Knowledge and Intellectual Knowledge

What can a human being do that nonrational animals cannot? What does intellectual (or rational) thinking mean?

To answer this, let us go back to Rover and his slice of pepperoni pizza. Rover smells the qualities of this particular slice of pizza, and his appetites are activated (that is, he feels love and desire) with regard to *this* individual piece of pizza.

We, being animals too, respond in a similar manner. But what we have, and what Rover does not have, is the capacity to know pizza in a different, higher way. Like Rover, we human beings are able to know individual pieces of pizza. But in addition to this, we can also grasp *what* pizza is; that is, we are able to know or grasp the *essence* of pizza.

Similarly, when I perceive Rover with my senses, I know him as a concrete individual. But if I think and use my reason, I can also grasp *what* Rover is, namely, that he is a dog. I can also look at Lassie and Snoopy and, with my intellect, I can grasp that they too are dogs. In other words, I can, with my intellect, understand *what* things are.

Now, an interesting feature about knowing *what* something is with my reason is that, in contrast with the senses that know individuals, I form a *concept* or *idea* that applies to many individuals. Following the example of how I know Rover and what he is, this means that although I know Rover as an individual with my senses, the *essence* of dog that I grasp with my intellect is not an individual dog. Instead, what I have is an idea or concept of dog that is applicable not just to one individual but to many individuals (of the same sort).

To better understand this, let us consider the difference between my sense knowledge of individual dogs and my intellectual knowledge of the essence of "dog." When I look and sense Rover, I sense his particular color, size, shape, and so on. When I look at Lassie, I sense *her* particular colors, shape, and size. The same happens when I sense Snoopy.

Now, with my intellect, I can exercise a vital operation that goes beyond simply knowing these individual dogs. With my intellect, I can grasp *what* Rover is (which is a dog), *what* Lassie is (also a dog), and *what* Snoopy is (a dog). Thus, I am able to capture *what* they are; I am able to understand the *essence* of dog.

But what color is this essence of dog? What shape is it? What size? If we think about it, we realize that the essence of dog (which I know with my intellect) has, in itself, no particular color, shape, or size. And yet, at the same time, I can say that Rover, Lassie, and Snoopy are all dogs.

If, with my senses, I have knowledge of individuals, how can I describe this knowledge of essences that I have with my reason? Aquinas, following Plato and Aristotle, calls this type of understanding *knowledge of universals* (in contrast with the knowledge of individuals that I get with my senses). This helps us better understand the difference between sense knowledge (which all animals have) and intellectual knowledge (which only rational animals like human beings have). Generally speaking, with our senses we know individual material beings and their sensible qualities. But with our intellects, we can capture *what* that material being is, and this knowledge applies to many individuals of the same kind (it is knowledge of a universal idea).[2]

This distinction between sense knowledge and intellectual knowledge is crucial to understanding what makes human beings specifically distinct from other animals. As Aquinas puts it, human beings are animals (we are living beings with senses and appetites), but what makes us a different kind of thing from all the other animals is that we have the power of reason, which is the capacity to have universal knowledge of the essences of material things.[3]

---

2. "The soul, through the intellect, has cognition of bodies by means of a cognition that is immaterial, universal, and necessary." Aquinas, *Summa Theologiae* 1.84.1.

3. "For a rational nature exceeds a sentient nature with respect to *the object of cognition*, since there is no way in which a sensory power can have a cognition of a universal, which is what reason has cognition of." Aquinas, *Summa Theologiae* 1-2.5.1.

The Intellect and Its Operation

The passive intellect, its first operation, and its object

Now that we have an initial sense of what intellectual knowing is and of how it differs from sense knowing, we need to take a more systematic look at the power or capability of intellectual knowing, its basic operation, and its object.

In chapter 3, we characterized the power of sight as the capability for an operation (more specifically, for seeing), which in turn concerns some aspect of reality that is its object (in this case, color). We now need to do the same for intellectual knowing.

First, the *power* or *faculty*. Just as the operation of seeing requires a power or capacity to see, there is a power or capacity to intellectually know essences. Aquinas calls this power the *passive intellect* (in contrast to the active or agent intellect that we will study later).

Next, the *operation*. As we shall see, the intellect is capable of executing several types of intellectual operations. In the previous section, we focused only on one of these: the intellectual knowing by which we know the essence of something. This basic and initial intellectual knowing is called *simple apprehension*. Subsequent operations, such as the speculative intellect's judgment and reasoning and the practical intellect's operations (including inquiry and deliberation), will be studied later.

Finally, the *object*. As we see above, by performing the operation of intellectual knowing (simple apprehension), the intellect knows the essences of things. And thus, the object of intellectual knowing is the *essence* or the *quiddity* (the *what*) of material things.[4]

4. "In the state of the present life the object of our intellect is the 'whatness' of a material thing, which the intellect abstracts from the phantasm." Aquinas, *Summa Theologiae* 1.85.8.

With this, we can summarize intellectual knowing by comparing it with the power of sight. Just as the **power of seeing** (=power) *sees* (=operation) COLOR (=object), the **passive intellect** (=power) *simply apprehends* (=operation) the ESSENCES OF MATERIAL THINGS (=object).

The agent intellect, illumination, and abstraction

Although all this seems simple, there is one other element that we need to consider; namely, the intellectual light that Aquinas calls the agent or active intellect.

One simple way to understand this light of the intellect is to compare it to the physical light that accompanies the act of seeing colors. To see a color, there must first be a sensible quality in the thing that we are sensing. There also needs to be an organism capable of seeing (that is, one that has the power of sight). The act of seeing the color comes about when the sensible quality that is in the external thing alters the physical organ of the sense power of seeing (the eye and the visual system of the brain). This alteration then moves the power of seeing from potentially seeing to actually seeing, and it is at this point that the power of seeing sees the color.

Something analogous happens with intellectual knowing. First, there is an essence that can be known (analogous to color). Then there is the power that is capable of knowing essences, which is the passive intellect (analogous to the power of sight).

There are, however, some differences between seeing colors and intellectually "seeing" essences that we must point out.

The first concerns light. Although the color of a thing is a quality that is sensible in the thing, the power of sight needs light if it is to be able to see that color. Along the same lines, a material being has an essence that can be "seen" by the intellect, but just as the power of sight needs physical light to see the color of a thing, the intellect needs a "light" to "see" the essence of material beings. This *intellectual light* is what Aquinas calls the *active* or *agent intellect*.[5]

The second concerns how we obtain universal concepts. In chapter 3, we saw how knowledge of individual material beings begins with the external senses, which capture the sensible qualities of things, and continues with the internal sense, especially the imagination, which organizes all previous sensory input into a unified perception (called an image or phantasm). It is, therefore, in the operation of the imagination that the animal comes to have knowledge of a concrete individual being.

Intellectual knowing, however, is knowledge of the essence of a thing, which is not individual but universal. How do we pass from sensible knowledge of individual things (in the phantasm of the imagination) to knowledge of an essence that is universal? Aquinas answers that what is needed is that the agent intellect, aside from being intellectual light, also *abstracts* the essence from the individuating material conditions of the individual thing.[6] For example, from the perception of Rover,

---

5. "Just as light is necessary for seeing something, so the active intellect is necessary for understanding something intellectively." Aquinas, *Summa Theologiae* 1.79.3.

6. "What belongs to the nature (*ratio*) of any species of material thing, e.g., *rock* or *man* or *horse*, can be considered without the individual principles, which do not belong to the nature (*ratio*) of the species. And to abstract the universal from the particular, or to abstract the intelligible species from the phantasms, is just this: to consider the nature (*natura*) of the species without considering the individual principles that are represented through the phantasms." Aquinas, *Summa Theologiae* 1.85.1.

"And the active intellect *abstracts* the intelligible species from the phantasms in the sense that (a) by the power of the active intellect we are able, in our

with his individualizing characteristics (his color, size, shape, and so on), the intellect abstracts the universal essence of dog. The same could be said when I sense Lassie with her own individual qualities. With my agent intellect, I *illuminate* the phantasm of Lassie that I have in my imagination (thereby making her essence as dog "seeable" by the passive intellect), and then I *abstract* her essence from her individual characteristics.[7] Once this is done, the passive intellect passes from potentially knowing Lassie's essence to actually knowing it with the operation of simple apprehension.

Indirect knowledge of the individual by the intellect

Since the essence of material beings entails that in reality (that is, outside the mind), they exist as individual beings, perfect knowledge of these essences would then require knowledge of individuals as well. This means that if the intellect is to have perfect knowledge of the essence of a material being, it needs to know individuals somehow. A consequence of this is that, according to Aquinas, once the intellect grasps the universal essence of a thing, it turns back to the phantasm from which it abstracted this essence. By doing so, it is able to understand the universal essence (that it knows with simple apprehension) as existing in a concrete individual (by turning back to the

---

thinking, to grasp the natures of the species without their individual conditions, and that (b) the passive intellect is informed by the likenesses of these natures." Aquinas, *Summa Theologiae* 1.85.1.

See also Aquinas, *Summa Theologiae* 1.79.2.

7. "It is the case both that (a) the phantasms are illuminated by the agent intellect and, again, that (b) the intelligible species are abstracted from them by the power of the active intellect." Aquinas, *Summa Theologiae* 1.85.1.

concrete phantasm in the imagination).[8] Aquinas calls this an *indirect knowledge* of the individual by the intellect (in contrast to its *direct knowledge* of essences).

To go back to our example, with simple apprehension I can understand the essence of dog, and I do so by abstracting that essence from the phantasm of Rover that I have in my imagination. But since real dogs are always individual dogs, to really understand what a dog is I need to turn my intellect to an individual dog, which I do by turning it back to the concrete phantasm of Rover that I have in my imagination. And once I do this, I can form the proposition, "This (Rover) is a dog."

The Continuation of Intellectual Thought

The speculative reason and the practical reason

Aside from simple apprehension and the return to the concrete phantasm, the intellect carries out a number of other operations. Some of these operations involve simply knowing the truth, and these are what Aquinas calls operations of the

---

8. "It is part of the conception of the nature of a rock that it exists in individual rocks (*de ratione naturae lapidis est quod sit in hoc lapide*), and part of the conception of the nature of a horse that it exists in individual horses, and so on for the others. Hence, the nature of a rock, or of any material entity, is such that there cannot be a complete and true cognition of it except insofar as it is thought of as existing in a particular. But we apprehend particulars through the sensory power and the imagination. And so for the intellect to have an actual intellective understanding of its own proper object, it is necessary that it turn itself to phantasms, in order that it might inspect the universal nature as it exists in the particular." Aquinas, *Summa Theologiae* 1.84.7.

"Our intellect has direct cognition only of the universals. . . . However, our intellect can have cognition of the singular indirectly and, as it were, by a sort of turning back." Aquinas, *Summa Theologiae* 1.86.1.

speculative intellect.[9] These include the operations of judgments (by which we formulate propositions) and reasoning (by which we reason from propositions to conclusions) that lead to the development of the speculative sciences (philosophy of nature, mathematics, and metaphysics).[10]

Other operations involve reasoning that leads to practical action (either making things or ethical action), and these belong to the *practical intellect*,[11] which we will study in chapters 6, 7, and 8.

The Immortality of the Rational Soul

The distinction between sensible knowledge (of individuals) and intellectual knowledge (of essences) implies an important distinction between the sense powers and the intellectual power, which, in turn, points to an essential difference between nonrational animal souls and rational ones. This difference also explains how the souls of rational animals can survive biological death.

The distinction between nonrational and rational souls can be seen in how their operations and objects differ. In chapter

9. See Aquinas, *Summa Theologiae* 1.79.11.

10. "The human intellect does not immediately come to a perfect cognition of a thing in its first apprehension of it. Instead, it first apprehends an aspect of it (*aliquid de ipsa*), viz., the 'what-ness' (*quidditas*) of the thing itself, which is the first and proper object of the intellect; and then it comes to understand the properties, accidents, and relations associated with the thing's essence. . . . Accordingly, it must necessarily (a) compose one apprehended thing with another or divide one apprehended thing from another and (b) proceed from one composition or division to another, i.e., reason discursively." Aquinas, *Summa Theologiae* 1.85.5.

"So the human intellect engages in intellective cognition by composing and dividing, as well as by reasoning discursively." Aquinas, *Summa Theologiae* 1.85.5.

11. See Aquinas, *Summa Theologiae* 1.79.11.

3, we saw how the sensible cognizing powers (the external and internal sense powers) all involve a specialized physical organ of the body. We also saw that in order for the power to execute its operation, the physical organ of the power needs to be altered by the physical quality that is in the external thing. Although the sense operation is not in itself a physical process, it still requires a physical alteration of its sense organ. Feeling heat, for example, requires a physical alteration of my hand, even if the feeling of heat is not itself completely physical.

We see here that all the operations of the vegetative and animal souls work through powers linked to the body's physical organs. This intrinsic link to physical organs leads Aquinas to conclude that when death occurs (that is, when the body is no longer capable of sustaining life), a substantial change occurs whereby the plant or animal ceases to be what it is.

When a dog dies, for example, it ceases to be a dog, and, properly speaking, what remains cannot even be said to be a dog, but rather the carcass of what *was* a dog. In this case, there has been a change from being a dog (which, in Aquinas' view, entails being alive and acting as a dog) to some other sort of thing (which no longer has a principle of life; that is, which no longer has a soul).

What, then, happens to the dog's soul after death? From a Thomistic point of view, the answer is that, since while it was alive its reality or being intrinsically involved a physical body and organs, once that physical being ceases to be, the soul ceases to be too. In other words, the dog's soul does not persist after its death. The reasoning here is that since during its life, there does not seem to be any aspect of its life that is completely independent of the body's materiality and functioning, it follows that there is nothing about the soul that persists after the functioning of that animal.

But what if there is some sort of living being that exhibits vital operations that seem completely separable from bodily organs? Is there some sort of operation that is, in itself, completely immaterial? If there is, then there is a power of that being that is completely immaterial as well. And if this is so, then there is a part of that soul that can survive the organism's death.

For Aquinas, there is just such an operation, and it is found in rational animals when they exercise intellectual knowing. Although this knowing requires a phantasm of the imagination to illuminate and abstract from, this illumination and abstraction, as well as the operation by which it knows essences, are, in themselves, wholly immaterial.[12] It follows then that the passive and agent intellects, considered in themselves, are also completely immaterial. And since these are powers of the rational soul, we can conclude that the rational soul is incorruptible and thereby survives the death of the rational animal.

SUMMARY

1. Intellectual knowing is a knowing that is essentially different from sense knowing.
2. Through intellectual knowing, we know the essences of things.
3. Knowledge of essences is knowledge of universal concepts (they apply to several individuals of the same species).
4. The power to intellectually know essence is the passive intellect.
5. The first operation by which we know the essence of things is simple apprehension.

12. "Aristotle held that the intellect has an operation that it does not share with the body." Aquinas, *Summa Theologiae* 1.84.6.

6. The object of simple apprehension is the essence of material things (their quiddity or whatness).
7. In order to know an essence, the sensible image (or phantasm) in the imagination needs to be illuminated, which is done by a part of the intellect called the agent intellect.
8. In order to know an essence, it must also be abstracted from the individual characteristics of the individual known, and this is also done by the agent intellect.
9. The intellect can have indirect knowledge of an individual by turning back to the phantasm of the imagination.
10. The completely immaterial nature of intellectual knowing means that the rational soul involves a part that is completely immaterial as well (the intellect) and thus survives the death of the organism.

CHAPTER 6

Will

In *A Hidden Life*, also directed by Terrence Malick, Franz Jägerstätter, an Austrian farmer during World War II, is called to active duty but refuses to swear an oath of loyalty to Hitler. He is therefore imprisoned and mistreated, while his family is ostracized from their small community and derided. Nonetheless, he remains steadfast in his decision, even as everyone around him seeks to dissuade and convince him that his resistance and possible execution will do nothing to change the regime. As Jägerstätter seeks the strength to remain faithful to his conscience, he asks, "If God gives us free will, we're responsible for what we do, what we fail to do, aren't we?" It is a question that the film explores as we experience, together with Jägerstätter, the risks and the drama of human freedom and fidelity.

This chapter explores the power in human beings by which we are able to direct our lives according to what is true and to choose what we understand to be good.

The Will: Rational Appetite

Thomas Aquinas begins the second part of his *Summa Theologiae* (the part that is focused on what we would today call moral theology) by identifying what makes human beings distinct from other animals. The human being is, he says, "a principle of his own works in the sense of having free choice and power with respect to those works,"[1] and he "differs from the non-rational animals in that he is the master of his own acts."[2] He then states that this mastery comes through *reason* and *will*.[3] A little further on, Aquinas links dominion over one's acts with *free choice*, "which is a power of will and reason."[4] Free will, then, has to do with reason and with will. We studied reason in chapter 5, and now we consider the will.

To understand what the will is, we need to recall what a sensible appetite is. In chapter 4, we described a sensible appetite as a power of the soul. More specifically, it is a capacity to *tend* toward or away from material beings, tendencies that we call *feelings* or *passions*. We also saw that these feelings arise when the sensible appetite is presented with something that has been evaluated as being suitable or harmful to the animal. And finally, we saw that this evaluation of suitability is exercised not by the sensible appetite itself but by the estimative power, which is one of the internal sense powers of an animal.

Keeping all this in mind, we can understand how the will is an appetite as well. But it is an appetite that is activated not by a sensible good (as evaluated as such by the estimative power). Instead, it is activated by a thing or action that has been *judged to be good* by the *intellect*. Here, we need to point out that this judgment of the intellect is not simply the sensible operation of the estimative power that evaluates some particular thing as suitable or harmful, agreeable or disagreeable on a sensible level. Instead, the intellect's judgment of the goodness of a thing or action is a judgment *based on the universal notion of goodness*.[5]

1. Aquinas, *Summa Theologiae* 1-2.pr.
2. Aquinas, *Summa Theologiae* 1-2.1.1.
3. See Aquinas, *Summa Theologiae* 1-2.1.1.
4. Aquinas, *Summa Theologiae* 1-2.1.2.
5. See Aquinas, *Summa Theologiae* 1.59.1.

The intellect, therefore, is not simply instinctively evaluating whether some particular thing is pleasant or unpleasant, nor is it an instinctual evaluation of the suitability or harmfulness of something. It is instead a judgment that some thing or action *is* good (regardless of how I feel about it on a sensible level). I can, for example, judge that eating a piece of pepperoni pizza *is* something *good* to do, regardless of whether or not I *feel* desire for the pizza. I can even judge that it would be good to *not* eat the pizza, and to give it to my hungry grandmother (even though I might feel a desperate urge to eat it myself).

Once the intellect judges something as good (or evil), it is presented to the will. Just as the sensible appetite is activated by something evaluated by the estimative powers as suitable or harmful, the will (the intellectual appetite) is activated by something judged by the intellect as being good (or evil).[6] Also, just as the activations of the sensible appetite are the passions (eleven of them: love, desire, joy, hate, aversion, sorrow, hope, despair, courage, fear, and anger), the activations of the will are what we call *affections* and *other acts of the will* that have to do with ends and means. We will study these later in this chapter. For now, we can summarize what we have seen so far: (a) the will is a rational appetite (distinct from the sensible appetite); (b) the will is moved to act by a thing or action that has been judged by the intellect to be good; and (c) the will's operations include affections of the will and other acts of the will that have to do with ends and means.

Affections of the Will

When a nonrational animal perceives some sensible good, its sensible appetite is activated in the form of one of the eleven

6. See Aquinas, *Summa Theologiae* 1-2.8.1.

passions described in chapter 4. Similarly, when the will is presented with something judged to be good (or evil), it is activated in different ways as affections (not passions) of the will.

These affections parallel and have the same names as the passions of the sensible appetite. The objects of these affections of the will are, however, not particular sensible goods but rather goods apprehended by the intellect. Also, since the will, like the intellect, does not make use of a physical organ, these affections are immaterial and spiritual in nature. One consequence of this is that, although they are real inclinations to goods (or away from evils), they do not, in themselves, entail physical changes in the animal's body and are not, strictly speaking, experienced as feelings. This explains how one could, for example, *want* to do something (like focus on study) without necessarily *feeling* a desire to do so.[7]

As mentioned, the affections of the will parallel the passions of the sensible appetite, but with the difference that the affections refer to the good as apprehended by the intellect (not by the senses) and are, therefore, spiritual inclinations that are not necessarily felt. Like the passions of the sensible appetite, the specific affections that arise in the will depend on whether it is presented with a good or with an evil and whether that good or evil is immediate or difficult.

---

7. "Love (*amor*), concupiscence (*concupiscentia*), and other things of this sort are taken in two ways.

For sometimes they are taken insofar as they are certain passions, bringing with them a certain arousal of feeling (*cum concitatione animi*). This is the way they are commonly taken, and when they are taken in this way, they exist only in the sentient appetite.

In the second way, they signify a simple affection, without passion or an arousal of feeling. Taken in this way, they are acts of the will, and in this sense they are likewise attributed to the angels and to God." Aquinas, *Summa Theologiae* 1.82.5.

The affections of the will are, therefore, the following: (1) *love* (when the will is presented by a good apprehended by the intellect); (2) *desire* (when the will moves toward that good); (3) *joy* (when the will possesses what it was moving toward); (4) *hatred* (when the will is initially presented with an evil apprehended by the intellect); (5) *aversion* (when the will moves away from some evil); (6) *pain* or sorrow (when the will is in possession of some evil); (7) *hope* (when the will strives for something good, but difficult, yet seemingly attainable); (8) *despair* (when the will strives for some difficult good that begins to seem unattainable); (9) *courage* (when the will is confronted with an arduous evil that it might overcome); (10) *fear* (when the will is faced with a difficult evil that it might succumb to); and (11) *anger* (when the will seeks retribution for some evil inflicted on it).

Thus, for example, I might *love* the possibility of shopping for sales (an immediately accessible good), *desire* to actually go shopping, and *enjoy* actually shopping. Or I might *hate* scraping the ice off my car (an immediate evil), have *aversion* to actually doing so, and be *sad* as I do it. I might *hope* to make it to the top of Mount Everest if I'm only a few yards away (an arduous good that seems attainable) or *despair* about getting there because of heavy snow and ice (an arduous good that appears to be slipping from my grasp). On the other hand, I might have *courage* about defeating some sort of extraterrestrial monster (if I seem to be getting the upper hand) or be *fearful* about succumbing to it (if I accidentally slip and fall to the ground). And finally, I might be *angry* if I realize my business partner has been stealing from my portion of the profits. All these are affections of the will that are inclinations toward goods or away from evils that are real, even if I may not feel them as sensible passions.

Ends and Means

In practical activity, the good that the intellect apprehends is also said to be a goal or an *end* to be obtained through some sort of action. Thus, while the idea of getting into shape is something wanted by the will because it is seen as something good, it can also be said to be a goal or an end that the will seeks to attain.

Related to the notion of end is that of *means*. A means is something willed, not for its own sake but because it makes it possible to achieve something else. In Aquinas' understanding of action, ends are willed for their own sake (they are understood as goods in themselves). Means are also willed, though they are willed not for their own sake but for the sake of something else. For example, we normally do not take medicine just for its own sake. The *end* that we want is health, and we want to take medicine insofar as it is a *means* to obtaining health.

The distinction between ends and means can also lead to more complex orderings of action. In this regard, it is possible that an end can be taken as a means to some other end. Money, for example, is always a means to something else. It is a means, for example, by which we can purchase a movie production studio. Here, the end, or goal, is to have a movie studio, and the means to achieving that goal is money. But it is also possible to want a movie company for some other end—for example, to gain a good reputation in the movie industry. Thus, having a movie studio can be considered as a means to another end; namely, having a good reputation.

It is possible to go even further, since I might want a good reputation as a means to an even further end; for example, political power. In that case, having a good reputation in the movie industry is a means to political power (which is willed as an end).

Acts of the Will with Regard to Ends and Means

Ends and means can both be considered goods: ends are goods willed for their own sake, and means are goods willed for something else. As such, ends and means are objects of different acts of the will. Aquinas identifies three acts of the will that concern ends: *simple volition*, *intention*, and *enjoyment*.[8] He also lists three acts of the will that deal with means: *consent*, *choice*, and *use*.[9]

These acts of the will are best explained in relation to the different acts of the practical intellect that accompany them and by means of a concrete example. Let us consider a previous scenario, and start with the last end we mentioned: political power.

First, there is an act of the intellect by which I apprehend that political power is a good. Corresponding to this is the act of the will called *simple volition*, by which the *will simply wills a good* that I might possibly seek, and thus *as a possible end*.[10]

Next, I start to consider how I might achieve power, and I begin to see power as a goal toward which I order a number of activities. This end is now the object of another act of willing called *intending*.[11] Intending entails not just willing an end in a general, vague way, but also willing it as something I now begin to direct my actions toward (I *intend* it). In our example, when I decide I do want power, and I begin to consider what I need to attain it, I am now *intending* that end.

---

8. See Aquinas, *Summa Theologiae* 1-2.8.pr.

9. See Aquinas, *Summa Theologiae* 1-2.8.pr.

10. See Aquinas, *Summa Theologiae* 1-2.8–10.

11. See Aquinas, *Summa Theologiae* 1-2.12.

At this point, our consideration now passes to *how* I am going to attain my end; that is, I start to consider the means to this end and to determine which particular means I should use. Once I intend political power, I now begin to consider how I can achieve it and the means to attain it. For example, what are the paths to political power, and which is the one I should take? Is it having a social media presence, a Harvard education, writing a book, or owning a movie studio? The inquiry into the means is an act of the intellect called deliberation, and the act of the will by which I will this is called *consent*.[12] Consent involves something more than intending, since it includes the will to consider how I can actually achieve that end.

The deliberation of the practical reason must come to an end at some point, and this happens with another act of the practical intellect by which I judge (or determine) which means would be best to use at this particular moment and in this concrete situation. In our example, after having deliberated on the many ways to achieve political power, I might determine that the best path, given my particular personal situation, is to have a movie studio. Once I make this determination, there is an act of the will by which I freely *choose* that means.[13] In our example, this means that once I determine (after a period of study, consultation, and deliberation) that the way to go is to own a movie studio, I *choose* to go down that path.

Then, there is the intellect's command that orders something to be done and the act of the will called *use*, by which the will activates the executing powers to pursue the course of action that has been chosen.[14] In our example, use sets

12. See Aquinas, *Summa Theologiae* 1-2.15.

13. See Aquinas, *Summa Theologiae* 1-2.13.

14. See Aquinas, *Summa Theologiae* 1-2.16.

into motion all the actions necessary to obtain a movie production company.

Finally, once I have the movie studio, there is the act of the will called *enjoyment*, by which the will delights in the goal or end that it was striving to achieve.[15]

Acts of the Will and Particular Goods

An important characteristic of the will, which has a bearing on its acts, is that it is not moved with necessity by any *particular* good. If the will were presented with a thing or an action that is apprehended as "good in every respect and according to every way of thinking about it,"[16] the will would tend toward it necessarily. But, since no *particular* good is good in every respect, the will does not tend to any particular good with necessity. This is because every particular good "insofar as it is lacking in some good, is able to be thought of as not good, and in this respect it can be either rejected or accepted by the will, which is able to tend toward the same thing according to the different ways of thinking about it."[17] This non-necessity of the will's tending to a particular good has consequences for free choice, as we will see in the next section.

Free Will

Now is a good time to go back to our faithful friend Rover in a way that helps us better understand the will and its acts and

15. See Aquinas, *Summa Theologiae* 1-2.11.

16. Aquinas, *Summa Theologiae* 1-2.10.2.

17. Aquinas, *Summa Theologiae* 1-2.10.2.

how they differ from the sensible appetites and passions of nonrational animals.

The primary distinguishing feature of human beings is that we have reason. And because we have reason, we have a will that is *free*. Since we have what Aquinas calls perfect cognition, we can not only act but we can also act for the sake of an end.[18] This perfect cognition of an end entails that (a) we apprehend some thing or action as an end; (b) we understand it *as* an end; and (c) we have knowledge of the means as ordered to an end.

For Aquinas, this sort of knowledge belongs only to rational animals.[19] Nonrational animals, on the other hand, have knowledge of an end, but without knowing it *as* an end.

Rover, for example, knows a piece of pizza and evaluates it as something suitable and, therefore, as an end that he tends to with his sensible appetite (in the form of the passions of love and desire). Rover, however, comes to knowledge of this end by a kind of instinct—it is an evaluation done by the estimative powers, which is an internal sense power.[20] He therefore has knowledge of an end, but not *as* an end. I, on the other hand, have not only sensible knowledge and attraction to the piece of pizza. I can, in addition to this, consider with my reason whether or not eating the pizza is something good to do here and now. Thus, I judge eating the pizza *as* a good *and as* an end. And, once I know it as something good to do, I can freely *intend* to do it, *consent* to doing it, *choose* how to do it, and *execute* the actions needed to actually eat the slice of pepperoni pizza.[21]

---

18. See Aquinas, *Summa Theologiae* 1-2.6.1.

19. See Aquinas, *Summa Theologiae* 1-2.6.2.

20. See Aquinas, *Summa Theologiae* 1.59.3.

21. See Aquinas, *Summa Theologiae* 1-2.12.5, 1-2.13.2, 1-2.15.2, 1-2.16.2, and 1-2.17.2.

Moreover, since my will is not necessarily moved by the particular good of eating pizza, I am *free* to intend or not intend eating the pizza, to consent or not to consent to eating it, to choose or not to choose how to eat it, and to actually go about eating it or not. Rover, on the other hand, is not free to intend, to consent, to choose, or to go through with eating the pizza. Instead, he apprehends eating the pizza as an end or sensible good by instinct (and memory of past sensible experiences) and moves toward it insofar as he is inclined to the pizza by his passions—and thus, not freely.

SUMMARY

1. The will is a rational appetite.
2. Though the object of a sensible appetite is a particular sensible good (evaluated as such by the estimative power), the object of the will is a thing or an action that is judged by reason to be good.
3. The will tends toward the good apprehended by reason in the form of affections of the will.
4. The affections of the will include love, desire, joy, hate, aversion, sadness, hope, despair, courage, fear, and anger.
5. The good seen as the goal of actions is an end.
6. An end is something wanted for its own sake.
7. Means are wanted not for their own sake, but for something else.
8. The acts of the will with regard to ends are simple volition, intention, and enjoyment.
9. The acts of the will with regard to means are consent, choice, and use.

CHAPTER 7

Science and Craft

The fifth and last part of J. R. R. Tolkien's *The Silmarillion* describes the forging of the nineteen Rings of Power and the One Ring, which later go on to play a significant role in the later events of Middle Earth as recounted in *The Lord of the Rings*. Forging these rings required great knowledge of materials and lore, as well as great power and craft. Both the theoretical knowledge needed and the craft required had to be acquired through study and practice, and were passed from master to apprentice. This growth of knowledge and craft entails what Aquinas calls *habits* in general and, more specifically, *science* and *craft*.

For Aristotle and Aquinas, human action is characterized by the role that reason plays in it. This applies to the operations of reason itself (simple apprehension of essences, judgment, and reasoning) and to the acts of the will that have the good apprehended by reason as their object. It also applies to human sensible life, especially to the passions of the sensible appetite insofar as these operations are ordered by the rational part of the human soul. This chapter and the next examine the different types of human action that follow from reason and the perfecting of different powers by habits (the intellectual and moral virtues). This chapter discusses the habits that perfect reason with regard to speculation of the truth (what Aquinas calls *scientific knowledge*) and making things (which Aquinas calls *art* or *craft*). The next chapter will focus on moral action and the moral virtues (especially the virtue of *prudence*).

Habit and Virtue

Habit as perfection of a power

As we have seen, all living beings manifest their life through vital *operations* and *activities*. Rover, for example, is alive, but his life becomes manifest in his growing and eating; he also looks and sniffs around, and he responds to what he senses with a variety of feelings. The lives of human beings manifest themselves in similar ways, but they are also expressed in vital activities of the reason and of the will that go beyond animal life. All these operations are activities of capabilities that living beings have, capabilities that Aquinas calls *powers of the soul*.

One special characteristic of the powers proper to human beings (the power of intellect or reason, the will, and the powers of the sensible soul insofar as their operations can be ordered according to reason) is that they can act in different ways. They are, as Aquinas says, "able to be determined in more than one way" and "to diverse things."[1] But, although the rational powers are so indeterminate, they can acquire *stable dispositions* by which they can be disposed to act either well or badly.[2] Aquinas considers these stable dispositions toward certain operations as *perfections* (or degradations) of powers, and he calls them *habits*.

For Aquinas, "every power that can be ordered in diverse ways toward acting needs a habit by which it is well disposed toward its act."[3] Since these are the powers that have to do with

1. Aquinas, *Summa Theologiae* 1-2.49.4.
2. See Aquinas, *Summa Theologiae* 1-2.49.1.
3. Aquinas, *Summa Theologiae* 1-2.50.5.

reason, it follows that the powers that can be perfected by habits are (1) the reason;[4] (2) the will;[5] and (3) the powers of the sensible soul insofar as their operations can be ordered according to reason (which are principally the sensible appetites).[6]

Virtue

Habits can be good or bad. A habit is called good "when it disposes one to an act that is appropriate for the agent's nature." On the other hand, a habit is called bad "when it disposes one to an act that is inappropriate for the nature."[7]

This distinction allows us to understand what Aquinas means by virtue. For Aquinas, a human virtue is a good habit of one of the powers of the human soul mentioned above as being determined in more than one way to many acts. Thus, for Aquinas, a human *virtue* is a *good habit of the intellect, of the will, or of the sensible appetites*. As a *habit*, it is a *stable disposition* of these powers toward operations.[8] And as a *good* habit, it is a *perfection of those powers to acts that are appropriate to the nature of those powers and of human nature.*[9] Finally, since the acts that are appropriate to the nature of human beings are acts in accordance with reason, a human virtue is a "habit by which someone operates well";[10] that is, it is *a perfection of a human power that disposes it to operations in accordance with reason*.

4. See Aquinas, *Summa Theologiae* 1-2.50.4.

5. See Aquinas, *Summa Theologiae* 1-2.50.5.

6. See Aquinas, *Summa Theologiae* 1-2.50.3.

7. Aquinas, *Summa Theologiae* 1-2.54.3.

8. See Aquinas, *Summa Theologiae* 1-2.55.1.

9. See Aquinas, *Summa Theologiae* 1-2.56.1.

10. See Aquinas, *Summa Theologiae* 1-2.56.3.

Kinds of virtue

Since we have seen that the powers capable of being perfected in the way described above are the intellect, the will, and the sensible appetite, it follows that there are *intellectual virtues, a virtue of the will,* and *virtues that perfect the sensible appetite.*

Virtues of the Speculative Intellect

Truth

In chapter 5, we studied the human intellect and its first operation, which is simple apprehension by which we come to know the essence of a material being. When I see and smell an apple, I can know not just *this* particular apple, but I can, through the operation of simple apprehension (an operation of the intellect), come to know *what* it is; namely, that it is an apple. Here, we should note that knowledge of the essence of the apple entails a conformity of my intellect with the reality of the apple. This *conformity of intellect and reality* is the first sense of what Aquinas calls *truth.*[11]

Speculative intellect and practical intellect

The intellect's cognition of truth can, however, be ordered toward different ends. More specifically, *knowledge of truth can be ordered simply to the consideration of truth* without practical action, and this belongs to the dimension of the intellect that Aquinas calls the *speculative intellect*. On the other hand, *knowledge of truth can be ordered toward action*, and this pertains to

11. "The true exists in an intellect insofar as that intellect is conformed to the thing that is understood." Aquinas, *Summa Theologiae* 1.16.1.

"Truth is defined as a conformity between the intellect and the thing." Aquinas, *Summa Theologiae* 1.16.2.

the dimension of the intellect that Aquinas calls the *practical intellect.*[12] Practical intellect, in turn, can be directed either to *making* something external or to *moral action*.

The sections that follow will examine the habits of the speculative intellect and of the practical intellect with regard to making. We will consider the habits linked with moral action in the next chapter.

Judgment and reasoning

For Aquinas, the first operation of the intellect is *simple apprehension*, and it is through this activity that we come to have knowledge of *what* something is. This knowledge, however, is not a perfect cognition of the thing. More perfect knowledge of a thing comes with an understanding of the properties and relations associated with a thing's essence.[13] This additional knowledge is obtained by an operation of the intellect that continues beyond simple apprehension. Aquinas calls this operation "composing and dividing," and it has come to be known as *judgment*. Judgment is an operation of the intellect that composes one apprehended thing with another or divides one apprehended thing from another. It is a sort of comparison and contrasting of things and attributes.[14] For example, through simple apprehension, I can obtain the concepts of "dog" and "cactus," as well as the general notions of "animal" and "plant." With the operation of judgment, I can make propositions that put notions together or that divide them

12. "Practical understanding is ordered toward the end of effecting something, whereas the end of speculative understanding is the consideration of truth." Aquinas, *Summa Theologiae* 1.14.16. See also 1.79.11.

13. See Aquinas, *Summa Theologiae* 1.85.5.

14. See Aquinas, *Summa Theologiae* 1.85.5.

from each other. For example, "Dogs are animals" or "A cactus plant is not an animal."

After this, the intellect can proceed from one judgment to another by an operation called discursive *reasoning*. By reasoning, the intellect "proceeds from what is known to the investigation of things that are unknown."[15] In other words, the intellect starts with propositions that it already knows (called *premises*) and, by a process of reasoning (or *syllogism*), arrives at *a conclusion* that it did not know before.

For example:

"All animals have senses." (Premise 1)

"All dogs are animals." (Premise 2)

Therefore, "All dogs have senses." (Conclusion)

Or:

"All rational beings have free will." (Premise 1)

"All hobbits are rational beings." (Premise 2)

Therefore, "All hobbits have free will." (Conclusion)

Types of syllogism

The type of reasoning or syllogism and the certainty that one has of the conclusion depend on several factors. In the foreword to his commentary on Aristotle's *Posterior Analytics*, Aquinas identifies three types of syllogism.[16]

---

15. Thomas Aquinas, *Aristotle:* On Interpretation; *Commentary by St. Thomas and Cajetan*, trans. Jean T. Oesterle (Milwaukee, WI: Marquette University Press, 1962), Introduction.

16. See Thomas Aquinas, *Commentary on the* Posterior Analytics *of Aristotle*, trans. Fabian R. Larcher, OP (Albany, NY: Magi Books, 1970).

See also Aristotle, 1.1.100a24-100b20, Foreword.

The first type of reasoning is *demonstrative syllogism*. A demonstrative syllogism begins with *premises that are true and convincing in themselves.* It then leads to knowledge that is *necessary* (meaning that it cannot be otherwise) and *certain*. As we shall see, this type of knowledge leads to what Aquinas calls *scientia* (scientific knowledge).

A second type of reasoning is *dialectical syllogism*. This type of reasoning begins with "*reputable opinions*"—opinions that are accepted by everyone or by the majority or by the wise. Its conclusion involves something that is *true in most cases* (but not necessarily) and is *not always accompanied by certainty*. It, therefore, does not lead to science but rather to belief or opinions (in which reason leans completely to one side of a contradiction but with fear that the contrary side might be true).

And finally, there is *rhetorical argumentation*, which involves situations of suspicion in which reason does not lean to one side of a contradiction unreservedly, although it is inclined more to one side or another.

Virtues of the speculative intellect

A virtue is a good habit; that is, it is a perfection of a power that disposes it to act well. The speculative intellect, which orders its knowing to the contemplation of the truth, can be the subject of virtues insofar as these are habits that dispose the speculative intellect to act well (that is, to consider what is true well). Thus, a speculative intellectual virtue is "a virtue by which the speculative intellect is perfected in its consideration of what is true."[17] In this regard, Aquinas identifies three virtues of the speculative intellect: *understanding*, *scientific knowledge*, and *wisdom*.

17. Aquinas, *Summa Theologiae* 1-2.57.2.

To understand these intellectual virtues, we need to take another look at demonstrative syllogism, considering three stages of this type of syllogism.

First, this type of reasoning begins with *premises*, which are propositions that constitute the *starting points* (also called *principles*) of a syllogism or reasoning. In order for the syllogism to be demonstrative, these starting points or principles need to be *necessary* (meaning that they cannot be otherwise) and *certain*.

Second, starting with these principles or starting points, the reason, through *demonstrative syllogism*, arrives at a new proposition, which is the conclusion of that syllogism.

Third, the *conclusion* is also necessary and certain.

With this in mind, we can see how reason can be perfected by habits that dispose it in such a way that it knows the principles or starting points of demonstrations better, and so that it reasons to conclusions better.

The habit that perfects the speculative intellect so that it operates better with regard to starting points of areas of knowledge is what Aquinas calls *understanding* (Latin: *intellectus*). The habit of understanding is important because our reasoning about reality has to start somewhere—that is why the premises are called principles or starting points of reasoning. It is possible that the starting points of a particular syllogism may themselves be conclusions of previous syllogisms. But if this is so, those previous syllogisms would have to start with other earlier starting points. And if these earlier starting points are, in turn, conclusions of even earlier syllogisms, then those syllogisms would have to start with even more previous principles. Thus, at some point, we need to start with principles that are not the product of demonstration (otherwise, we keep going back infinitely).

In other words, reasoning must at some point have started with indemonstrable principles. It is here that understanding comes in as a perfection of the speculative intellect (a virtue) that enables reason to know indemonstrable principles that are the basis for reasoning about different aspects of reality.[18] For Aquinas, principles of this kind are immediately understood once we have knowledge of the essences of things. For example, once "we know what a whole and a part is, we grasp immediately that every whole is greater than its part."[19] Once we have knowledge of principles, we can reason to conclusions. If, as we have seen, the premises are necessary and certain, I can reason to a conclusion that I did not previously know, and which I know also as necessary and certain. By reasoning in this way, a more profound knowledge of things is formed in the intellect. It is this habit that perfects the speculative intellect with regard to knowledge obtained through demonstrative reasoning that Aquinas calls the virtue of *scientific knowledge* (Latin: *scientia*).[20]

One notable aspect of scientific knowledge of something is that I come to know not only *what* something is but also *why* it is what it is and how it came to be so. For example, most people have basic knowledge of pepperoni pizza that enables them to distinguish it from other types of pizza and maybe enough to form a preference for a particular pizza place. But someone who has studied pepperoni pizza has *scientific knowledge* of pizza and knows *why* pepperoni pizza is so good. He may, for example, know what pepperoni really is, what its

---

18. Understanding is a "particular habit by which a man, in virtue of the light of the active intellect, naturally knows indemonstrable principles." Thomas Aquinas, *Commentary on the* Nichomachean Ethics, trans. C. I. Litzinger, OP (Chicago: Regnery, 1964), 6.6.5.1179.

19. Aquinas, *Commentary on the* Nichomachean Ethics 6.6.5.1179.

20. "Science is a demonstrative habit, i.e., produced by demonstration." Aquinas, *Commentary on the* Nichomachean Ethics 6.3.3.1149.

chemical composition is, and how it reacts to melting cheese. As a result, he knows pepperoni pizza more profoundly than someone who does not have scientific knowledge, because he knows pepperoni pizza in light of causes and explanations of this kind of pizza.

Finally, there is the habit of *wisdom*. Wisdom perfects the speculative intellect so that it comes to know the highest realities, which are the principles and causes of all things. At the same time, it perfects reason so that it knows realities in the light of these principles. In this regard, wisdom is like understanding insofar as it involves knowledge of principles, and is like science insofar as it entails knowledge of things in the light of those principles.[21] Furthermore, for Aquinas, these higher principles or causes are realities that are beyond physical realities, and thus wisdom can be said to be the knowledge of what is beyond-physical, or *metaphysical*. Also, insofar as this ultimately includes knowledge that God exists and that he is the First Cause of all that is, wisdom is thus the study of God to the extent that our natural powers are capable and, therefore, can be called *natural theology*.

Virtues of the Practical Intellect with Regard to Making

Making

Earlier, we saw that the knowledge of truth that is obtained with the first operation of the intellect (simple apprehension) can be ordered either toward continued contemplation of the truth (which belongs to the speculative intellect) or toward

21. Thus, "wisdom, in declaring the truth about principles, is understanding; but in knowing the things inferred from the principles, it is science." Aquinas, *Commentary on the* Nichomachean Ethics 6.6.5.1183.

practical activity (which belongs to the practical intellect). In the previous section, we examined the virtues of the speculative intellect. Here, we will examine the virtues that perfect the practical reason with regard to making things.

For Aquinas, work, which entails *practical activity aimed at making things,* is part of human nature. If we observe other animals, they seem to have all they need to survive and flourish. They have, for example, fur to keep them warm and claws to defend themselves. On the other hand, humans seem to lack even the basic physical traits needed for survival. Aquinas responds to this in a surprising way. It is true, he says, that the bodies of human beings seem, at first glance, to be deficient with regard to physical attributes. But this is not entirely true, because nature has provided human beings with *reason* and *hands,* "by which he can make for himself, in an unlimited number of ways, weapons and coverings and the other things necessary for life."[22]

Here, we should consider three dimensions of the practical activity of making things.

First, making involves an operation of reason that is *ordered toward producing some external thing*. It is, therefore, a reasoning that aims not simply at thinking about the truth (as the speculative intellect does); it is, instead, ordered toward producing something external through the manipulation of material reality with our hands.[23] Making is thus "an operation passing into external matter to fashion something out

---

22. Aquinas, *Summa Theologiae* 1.91.3; see also 1.76.5 and 1-2.5.5.

23. "Reason produces certain things by way of making, in which case the operation goes out into external matter." Thomas Aquinas, *Commentary on Aristotle's* Politics, trans. Ernest L. Fortin and Peter D. O'Neill, "Sententia libri Politicorum," St. Isidore E-book Library, https://isidore.co/aquinas/Politics.htm, prol.6.

of it."[24] Two examples of making that Aquinas gives are construction and sawing.

Second, insofar as making involves the manipulation of external reality to produce something, it entails the *use of hands*.

Third, reason is not determined toward making just one thing or to making that one thing in just one way. Nor is there just one way to provide for a human being's needs. There are *many different things that can be made and many ways of doing so*. Because of our rational nature, human beings have "an unlimited number of ideas" and, as a result, we have the capacity to make, with our hands, "an unlimited number of instruments."[25]

Craft

Making involves not only the manipulation of external reality in an instinctive way. It requires the use of reason in different ways: for determining what kind of thing needs to be made in order to meet a need or demand; for understanding the properties of external reality and how it needs to be shaped in order to produce what is needed; for determining which instruments are needed to produce that thing; for understanding how to improve those processes; and so on.

Insofar as making involves the use of reason in these various areas of ordering and understanding, we can see how reason can be perfected so as to better go about making. The habit that disposes the practical intellect to better know how to make something is called the virtue of *craft* (Latin: *ars*, which is sometimes translated into English as "art"). As Aquinas puts it, craft is "a habit, concerned with making, under the guidance of reason."[26]

---

24. Aquinas, *Commentary on the* Nichomachean Ethics 6.3.3.1150.

25. Aquinas, *Summa Theologiae* 1.91.3.

In other words, craft is "right reason concerning certain works to be made."[27]

We should also add that a craft is a habit that is acquired through imitation and practice, and that it is aimed not only at producing something, but at making something well.[28]

Insofar as there are different kinds of things that can be made, there are different crafts. There are, for example, crafts that involve forging metal items (blacksmiths), building with stone (masons), making saddles (saddlemakers), preparing food (chefs), caring for a home, and so on.

SUMMARY

1. The rational powers (the intellect and the will) and the sensible appetite (insofar as their actions can be ordered according to reason) can be perfected by habits.
2. Virtues are good habits that perfect powers to dispose them to operate well.
3. Truth is conformity of intellect and thing.
4. The intellect's knowledge of truth can be ordered either to contemplation of the truth (operation of the speculative intellect) or to action (operation of the practical intellect).

---

26. Aquinas, *Commentary on the* Nichomachean Ethics 6.3.3.1153.

27. Aquinas, *Summa Theologiae* 1-2.57.3.

Also: "Now, there is a threefold operation of art: the first is to consider how an artifact is to be produced; the second is to operate on the external matter; the third is to accomplish the work itself. For this reason he says that every art is concerned with the creation, or the achievement and completion of the work which he places as the end of art." Aquinas, *Commentary on the* Nichomachean Ethics 6.3.3.1154.

28. See Aquinas, *Summa Theologiae* 1-2.57.3.

5. The virtues that perfect the intellect regarding consideration of the truth are called the virtues of the speculative intellect.
6. The virtues of the speculative intellect are understanding, science, and wisdom.
7. Making is an operation of the practical intellect that aims at making or producing an external thing.
8. The virtue of the practical intellect aimed at making something is called *craft*.

CHAPTER 8

Society, Happiness, and the Moral Virtues

In the *Analects*, the ancient Chinese philosopher Confucius (551–479 BC) presents the figure of the *junzi* (君子). *Junzi* literally means "noble man," but is here used by Confucius to signify an exemplary person, someone who has made significant progress in the *dao* (道, the Way). *Dao* is the path or the way of self-cultivation, on which one advances by developing specific habits or virtues such as a sense of justice (*yi* 義), propriety (*li* 禮), filial piety (*xiao* 孝), and trustworthiness (*xin* 信).[1] These classical Chinese virtues, which are to be cultivated throughout life, are fundamental manifestations and expressions of *ren* (仁). *Ren*, for its part, is a fundamental element in Chinese philosophical anthropology and ethical practice, and has been translated into English as perfect virtue, benevolence, goodness, humanness, love, or compassion. While it is an ethical principle within a person, it is not a specific virtue or practice. Instead, it is more like an innate capacity in all human beings to do good, something uniquely human that distinguishes human beings from other animals. *Ren* is both the inner source of good actions as well as an ethical ideal that the *junzi* strives to

1. See A. Charles Muller, comment on Confucius, *The Analects of Confucius*, trans. A. Charles Muller, "The Analects of Confucius 論語," rev. December 1, 2021, http://www.acmuller.net/con-dao/analects.html, 1.1.

cultivate within himself and in his social relationships, including governance of others.[2]

Similar notions of the ethical life, growth in virtue, and the importance of friendships and social life are also present in ancient Greek philosophers such as Socrates, Plato, and Aristotle. Their considerations of the ethical life and its relationship to God and supernatural revelation were later taken up and assimilated by medieval Islamic and Christian thinkers. In this chapter, we examine these topics within the context of the philosophical anthropology of Thomas Aquinas that we have been studying.

Society

A social-political animal

In chapter 7, we saw how human nature includes a dimension of practical activity aimed at making things and how Aquinas links making things with human needs. As we saw, although the human body seems to naturally lack specialized parts needed for survival (like fur or claws), Aquinas believes that nature has nevertheless provided human beings with reason and hands so that they can make what they need to survive. This human need to make what we need for survival also plays a role in Aristotle and Aquinas' understanding of why human beings naturally come together to form communities.

In his commentary on Aristotle's *Politics*, Aquinas states that a human being is *by nature* a *political being*,[3] and in

2. See Muller, comment on Confucius, 1.2.

3. Aquinas uses the phrase "homo sit naturaliter civile animal," which is typically translated as "man is by nature a political animal." Aquinas, *Commentary on Aristotle's* Politics 1.1.34. The Greek passage from Aristotle reads ὁ ἄνθρωπος φύσει πολιτικὸν ζῷον (*politikon zoon*). Aristotle, *Politics* 1.2.1253a2-3.

his commentary on Aristotle's *Nichomachean Ethics*, he describes the human being as a *social animal*.[4] He then goes on to show how we form different kinds of social groups in order, first of all, to find help to meet our basic needs and then to live well.[5]

The first community that forms is the *family*, which arises from the relationship between a man and a woman who come together by a natural desire to have children. It is a "society set up according to nature for everyday life, that is, for the acts that have to be performed daily," such as "eating, warming oneself at the fire, and others like these."[6]

When several families come together and aim at something more than the supply of daily needs, a *village* is naturally formed.[7] And then, from the union of several villages, the *city* comes into existence.[8] A city is a self-sufficient society that originates from the need to provide for the basic needs of life, but which is not limited to those and instead continues for the sake of the good life. A city thus has everything that is needed not only to live, but also to live well.

Ordering of activities within society

According to Aristotle and Aquinas, human beings *naturally* come together to form families, villages, and cities, and they do so because no one individual can provide for all his individual

---

4. See Aquinas, *Commentary on the* Nichomachean Ethics 1.1.1.4.

5. "It must be understood that, because man is by nature a social animal, needing many things to live which he cannot get for himself if alone, he naturally is a part of a group that furnishes him help to live well." Aquinas, *Commentary on the* Nichomachean Ethics 1.1.1.4.

6. Aquinas, *Commentary on Aristotle's* Politics 1.1.26.

7. See Aquinas, *Commentary on Aristotle's* Politics 1.1.27–28.

8. See Aquinas, *Commentary on Aristotle's* Politics 1.1.31.

needs. Thus, human beings come together to form societies to help one another first to survive and then to flourish.

Within each society, whether it be the basic family unit or a complex city, each individual who is part of that community performs different functions and activities. Many of these activities involve different kinds of making, and each one is interconnected with all the other activities of making that are present in that society. These making activities give rise, in turn, to various crafts or arts. These arts interact and intertwine with each other to provide for the various needs of the human beings within a given society. Aquinas gives as an example bridle-making and saddle-making, both of which are related to the art of horse-riding. Horse-riding, in turn, is just one of the various arts that are subordinated to the art of waging war.[9] Today, we might speak, for example, of moviemaking, political organization, banking, electric-vehicle production, homemaking, and pizza-making.

Each one of the activities of making within a society is directed toward an end (which is either the exercise of an activity or something produced by an activity). Then, as we saw in chapter 7, each of these ends is either desired for its own sake or as a means for some other end. For example, the art of pizza-making (along with the specific sub-art of pepperoni-pizza-making) requires other arts that act as means that make pizza-making possible. Among these could be the arts of furnace-making and bricklaying (specialties within the art of masonry), or dough-making and pepperoni-making. Pizza-making, in turn, might be a means to some further end or art, such as the art of restaurant services.

Now, faced with such a diversity of practical activity that we find in a complex society like a city, a question arises as to what all these activities are for and how they should be

9. See Aquinas, *Commentary on the* Nichomachean Ethics 1.1.1.16.

ordered (if they need to be ordered at all). It also brings up the question concerning the ethical activity of individual human beings within society. That is, aside from the aim of society in general, what is the goal or meaning of individual human lives?

Happiness

In the preceding chapters, we have seen the various powers and vital operations that form part of human living. Human beings eat and grow, sense colors and sounds, evaluate whether something is beneficial or harmful on a sensible level, understand the essences of things, reason about them, increase in knowledge, will, set goals (ends), deliberate about means to ends, choose, make use of things, and make things. Just as we asked how the various activities within a city are ordered and organized, we need to consider questions regarding the ordering of these multiple activities of human life and whether or not there is some overall meaning or goal toward which we should direct all our actions. If there is just such a goal or end, we must also consider what actions lead to (or lead away from) that end.

Final end

In chapter 6, we saw that an action or a thing can be desired either as an end for its own sake or as a means to something else. For Aristotle and Aquinas, money, for example, is something that is always desired for something else (for buying pizza, for example). Pepperoni pizza might, for its part, be wanted simply for its own sake (for example, because I like making pizza). But it is usually desired for the sake of something else (as a means to some other end). I can want pizza in order to eat it, for example. Or I might want it so that I have something to feed my ever-hungry teenage son. Or I might want to make money so that I can purchase a movie studio so that I can have political power. And so on.

With this example, we can see that although I sometimes want an activity or a thing for its own sake, I can still want it as a means to some other end. But can this be said for every possible end? Or is there an end that is desired for its own sake and can never be wanted as a means to some other end? If there is just such a thing or activity, then it would be an *end* beyond which there would be no other end, and as such, it would be an *ultimate* or *final* end.[10]

Aristotle and Aquinas argue that in human life there must be just such an end and that it would be the *end for which anything else is wanted*, and the *end that orders all other ends*.[11] Aquinas calls this final or ultimate end *happiness*.[12]

Happiness

If human life has a final end that orders all activity and toward which we direct all our operations, and if this is happiness, then we must now ask what happiness consists of.[13]

---

10. "Whenever an end is such that we wish other things because of it, and we wish it for itself and not because of something else, then that end is not only a good end, but a supreme end." Aquinas, *Commentary on the* Nichomachean Ethics 1.2.2.19.

11. "It follows that there must be some ultimate end on account of which all other things are desired, which this end itself is not desired on account of anything else." Aquinas, *Commentary on the* Nichomachean Ethics 1.2.2.22.

12. See Aquinas, *Commentary on the* Nichomachean Ethics 1.7.9.111.

13. We should note here that we are focusing on the happiness that is attainable in this life, which Aquinas calls "imperfect happiness." For Aquinas, "perfect happiness," which consists in the contemplation of the essence of God (the beatific vision), is not attainable by a human being's natural powers alone and requires a supernatural grace that elevates human nature and makes it capable of seeing God face-to-face.

Aquinas, following Aristotle, identifies happiness with some sort of *vital activity or operation*. But what kind of activity? Aquinas and Aristotle reason that happiness must be an *activity that is proper to human beings*, and since what sets human beings apart from other animals is reason, it follows that happiness consists of some sort of *activity of reason*.[14] Furthermore, insofar as appetites have operations that can and should be ordered in accordance with reason, happiness would also entail the operations of these powers insofar as they are properly disposed to follow reason. And since this involves their perfection through habits that we call *moral virtues*, happiness then requires the activity of the will (as perfected by the virtue of justice) and of the sensible appetites (as perfected by the virtues of fortitude and temperance).[15] In brief, *happiness consists in acting according to virtue*:

> If, therefore, man's proper role consists in living a certain kind of life, namely, according to the activity of reason, it follows that it is proper to a good man to act well according to reason and to the very good man or the happy man to do this in superlative fashion. . . . If the activity of the very good man or the happy man is to act well, in fact, to act to the best of his ability according to reason, it follows that the good of man, which is happiness, is an activity according to virtue.[16]

14. See Aquinas, *Commentary on the* Nichomachean Ethics 1.7.10.119.

15. "Moral virtue perfects the appetitive part of the soul by ordering it toward the good of reason." Aquinas, *Summa Theologiae* 1-2.59.4; "Reason not only orders the passions of the sentient appetite, but also orders the operations of the intellective appetite, i.e., the will." Aquinas, *Summa Theologiae* 1-2.59.4.

16. Aquinas *Commentary on the* Nichomachean Ethics 1.7.10.128.

Moral Virtues

If happiness is the ultimate end or goal of human life, and if it is for its sake that I desire everything else, then *how* do I attain it? What are the means (the things or actions) that I need if I am to attain happiness? To answer this, we need to consider two aspects of happiness as described in the preceding section: that happiness consists of (1) contemplation of the highest causes and principles; and (2) the exercise of operations of the appetitive powers in accordance with reason.

Regarding the contemplation of the highest causes, we saw in chapter 7 that this belongs to the exercise of the speculative intellect as perfected by the habit of wisdom. In this regard, happiness requires acquiring the intellectual virtue of wisdom, which is obtained through learning, discovery, and experience.

With regard to the performance of operations of the appetitive powers in accordance with reason, we need to consider the use of the practical reason with respect to voluntary acts that lead us to happiness and then its relationship to the acts of the rational appetite (the will) and the sensible appetite.

The practical intellect and the virtue of prudence

In chapter 7, we explored how the intellect's knowledge of truth can be ordered to the contemplation of truth or how it can be directed toward operations of making, which go out into things external to the organism. We now examine another side of the practical intellect, one that is directed not to operations of making that involve going out into external things, but rather to the ordering of voluntary acts that result in moral virtues and their exercise and contribute to attaining our final end (happiness).[17] The practical reason, insofar as it needs to determine which actions lead toward happiness and how virtue should be exercised in any given particular circumstance, can be the subject of a virtue that perfects it in its operation. Aquinas calls this the moral virtue of *prudence*. If craft is the virtue of the practical intellect that concerns making, prudence is the virtue of the practical intellect that perfects it with regard to *moral action*.[18] Unlike the operations of making, moral actions remain within the agent, and it is by repeated good moral actions that we develop stable dispositions in the appetites that we call the *moral virtues*. Aquinas likens the repetition of good moral acts that results in stable moral virtues in the appetites to the action of drops of water on stone that hollow it out over time.[19]

The will and the virtue of justice

In chapter 6, we saw that the will exercises a number of operations, including affections with regard to goods apprehended by the intellect and acts concerning various ends and means. For Aquinas, the will of each individual human being naturally wills what has been apprehended by a judgment of the intellect as being something good for that individual. In this case, the will does not need to be perfected by a habit in order to will what is good for the person. For example, if I haven't eaten for two days and I find a piece of pepperoni pizza on the table, I

17. See Aquinas, *Summa Theologiae* 1-2.57.4.

18. See Aquinas, *Commentary on the* Nichomachean Ethics 1.1.1.13; and Aquinas, *Summa Theologiae* 1-2.56.3 and 1-2.57.4.

19. See Aquinas, *Commentary on the* Nichomachean Ethics 2.1.1.249, where we also find the following passage: "We are perfected in these virtues by use, for when we act repeatedly according to reason, a modification is impressed in the appetite by the power of reason. This impression is nothing else but moral virtue."

not only crave that pizza with my sense appetite but I also judge with my practical intellect that it would be good for me to eat the pizza, and my will follows this apprehension by willing and choosing to eat the pizza.

There are, however, specific actions that I understand as being good to do that concern not my own good but the good of some other person. This takes on the form of being able to understand with my reason what good is due to another person. This judgment of a good to be done for someone else is presented to the will, which then can freely choose to do that good or not. Here, the will is capable of being perfected so that it is more disposed to want what is due to someone else; that is, it can acquire a perfection or habit that disposes it in a stable manner to will what is due to another person. This habit of the will is what Aquinas calls the moral virtue of *justice*.

The sensible appetites and the virtues of fortitude and temperance

Next, we need to consider the sense appetites and their operations (which are the sensible passions or feelings). In chapter 4, we saw how the sense appetites are activated as passions when presented with something that has been evaluated as suitable or harmful to the organism. In this sense, the passions naturally arise without any intervention of the reason or the will. In non-rational animals, this also means that they are moved to actions and things by their passions. Rational animals, however, are moved by goods understood and ordered by reason and freely intended, chosen, and executed by the will. This means that the passions of our sensible appetites can and should be influenced and ordered by reason.[20] We can, for example, overcome

20. See Aquinas, *Summa Theologiae* 1-2.59.1.

our intense desire for a piece of pepperoni pizza and choose to give it to Grandma (even though we may continue to crave it). Or, even though we fear bodily harm, we can decide to stand up against a situation of injustice.

Thus, insofar as the passions of the sensible appetite should be ordered by the rational powers, it too is capable of a stable perfection that disposes it to act in accordance with reason.[21] The habit that perfects the concupiscible sense appetite (whose passions are love, desire, joy, hate, aversion, and sadness) is the moral virtue of *temperance*. The habit that perfects the irascible sense appetite (whose passions are hope, despair, courage, fear, and anger) is the moral virtue of *fortitude*.

Growth and Perfection

One important consequence of the Aristotelian and Thomistic understanding of happiness is that it is never fully attained (at least in this life). If happiness consists in consideration of the highest truths and the exercise of virtues, and if we can always grow in the habit of wisdom and the moral virtues, it follows that our capacity for happiness can always grow. An indication of this is the subtle but clear distinction between what Aquinas calls a "good man" and a "very good man" (which also can be translated as "optimal man") that we saw earlier. For him, a "good man" acts well according to reason, while the "optimal man" (the happy man) does this in a *superlative* fashion. A similar distinction is found in Confucius. There is, on the one hand, the *junzi*, who is already quite advanced in expressing *ren* (or goodness) and thus can be considered closer to Aquinas' "optimal man." Yet, he too can grow since he has not yet attained

21. See Aquinas, *Summa Theologiae* 1-2.56.4.

the level of sage (*shengren* 聖人), who is considered almost as a divine being (a saint or enlightened one).[22]

SUMMARY

1. Human beings are social and political animals and, as such, naturally form societies.
2. The basic society is the family, which arises from the union of a man and a woman and provides for its members' basic, everyday needs.
3. A village arises from several families.
4. The city comes into existence from several villages, and it provides not just what its members need to survive but also what they need to live well.
5. A city provides for the various needs of its members through interconnected and hierarchically ordered activities and crafts.
6. Human life has an ultimate end, which is an end desired for its own sake and never for another; it is the end for which all other ends are wanted.
7. The ultimate end of human life is happiness.
8. Happiness consists in the exercise of virtue (contemplation of the highest truths and the exercise of moral virtue).
9. The virtue that perfects the practical intellect with regard to determining what good must be done in any given particular circumstance is prudence.
10. The virtue that perfects the will so that it is better disposed to will what is due to another is justice.

22. See Muller, comment on Confucius, 1.1.

11. The virtue that perfects the irascible sense appetite so that it acts in accordance with reason is fortitude.
12. The virtue that perfects the concupiscible sense appetite so that it acts in accordance with reason is temperance.
13. We can continually grow in wisdom and in the moral virtues.

CHAPTER 9

Person

Who Am I?

Another one of Terrence Malick's films, *The Tree of Life*, begins with a field of sunflowers under a brilliant sun as we hear a woman's voice saying, "There are two ways through life: the way of nature and the way of grace. You have to choose which one you'll follow." Who is this woman? Who is she talking to? Is she talking to us? Maybe she is talking to herself. But if she is, why would she talk to herself? Who is she talking to when she is talking to herself? Who am I talking to when I write these words? Am I talking to you? Or am I talking to myself? And . . . what is a self? *Who* is a self? This chapter and the next are about this self, this *I* that I am and that I talk to when I talk to myself.

Up until this point, we have been examining life and living beings from what we might call an external or third-person perspective. Even though we have often mentioned or described personal experiences such as a thought or a feeling, our characterization and explanation of these activities have mainly been in terms of objective notions and structures such as powers, operations, and habits. Such an approach presupposes the reality of, for example, feelings or thoughts, but theorizes about them within a conceptual framework that is at least one step removed from the immediate reality that it studies. Love, for example, is objectively described as a passion of the concupiscible sense appetite that arises when an animal evaluates something that it perceives as suitable for it (that is, as an immediate sensible good). Although this approach is true (it conforms to reality), it is also not exactly identical to the lived experience of love itself.

The question regarding the relationship between intellectual knowledge of a particular thing and concrete vital operations becomes more pressing when we are dealing with the personal experiences of rational beings (thoughts, feelings, affections) and their knowledge of their inner selves. We might ask, for example, if my personal experience of longing for chocolate ice cream is just a feeling of my sensible appetite, or if it involves an inner reality as well. And what about my freedom with respect to how much of it I eat? Is that just an operation of my practical intellect (which judges the appropriate amount I should eat) and of an operation of the will (by which I choose to eat just a certain amount)? And then, even more profoundly, what does this say about my self? Is my self reducible to simply a number of vital operations? Or is there a self that underlies all those activities? If there is, what is the nature of that self? How can I know that self? To what extent can I truly know the who that I am?

Questions about the self and how we can know ourselves have, of course, been asked throughout the history of thought. Oftentimes they have been raised within a religious context and experience, as was the case with Augustine and Pascal. At other times, they make their appearance within moments of existential questioning and the consideration of death, as with Kierkegaard and Heidegger and other existential thinkers of the twentieth century. These more modern and contemporary philosophical approaches to the human person and her intimacy differ in important ways from the Aristotelian-Thomistic perspective that we have taken in the first eight chapters of this book.

In this chapter, we will first consider the Thomistic notion of person and of self-knowledge. This is followed by a brief overview of the philosophical currents in modern and contemporary philosophy that gave rise to twentieth-century attempts at developing a philosophy of human subjectivity and the person. We will then examine the approaches of Karol Wojtyła, Joseph Ratzinger, and Leonardo Polo, which will give us a sense of how our study of the human person can expand upon and enrich the Aristotelian-Thomistic philosophical anthropology that we have been studying.

Person and Knowledge of Self in Aquinas

Person in Aquinas

For Aquinas, living beings are material substances with souls and, as such, carry out vital operations. Among living beings, rational beings have a special dignity and are called *persons*. Aquinas, following the sixth-century philosopher Boethius, describes a person as an "individual substance with a rational nature."[1] With this, Aquinas emphasizes that (a) a person is an *individual* (not just a general notion); (b) insofar as we are individuals, being a human person entails having a *particular body* (in Aquinas' terminology, we are individualized by having *this* flesh and *these* bones, as distinct from the flesh and bones of some other individual); and (c) as rational beings, we have free will by which we can direct ourselves to our ends, and thus also enjoy a special dignity.[2]

1. Aquinas, *Summa Theologiae* 1.29.1.

2. "There is an even more special and perfect mode in which particulars and individuals are found among *rational substances*, which have dominion over their acts and which are not just acted upon like other substances, but act on their own." Aquinas, *Summa Theologiae* 1.29.1.

Knowledge of the self in Aquinas

Having defined what *person* means, we now ask: How do persons come to know themselves? In chapter 5, we considered the intellect, which is the power of the soul by which a human being is capable of intellectually knowing. We also saw that the primary object of the intellect's operation (what the operation primarily concerns itself with) is the essence of material things. The question now arises as to how I know myself—since this is not a type of knowledge obtained by abstracting from sense knowledge and thus not the object of the intellect's first operation, which is simple apprehension of essences. For Aquinas, knowledge of self is related to understanding how the intellect comes to know itself, its habits, its operations, and the operations of the will.

As we just recalled, Aquinas considers the intellect as the capacity or power to know the essences of material things. It is not, however, always actually knowing something. But when it *is* knowing something, the intellect is actualized, and it is then that it is possible for the intellect to know itself through its operation as the principle from which that operation arises.[3] The same applies to how we come to know the intellect's operations and habits,[4] as well as the operations of the will.[5]

---

3. "But there is another type of intellect, viz., the human intellect, which (a) is not its own act of understanding and which (b) is such that the primary object of its act of understanding is not its own essence but instead something extrinsic, viz., the nature of a material thing. And so what is understood in the first place by the human intellect is an object of this latter sort, and what is understood in the second place is the very act by which the [primary] object is understood. Furthermore, by this act the intellect itself is understood, since the intellect's perfection is the very act of intellective understanding. This is why the Philosopher says that objects are understood prior to their acts, and acts prior to their powers." Aquinas, *Summa Theologiae* 1.87.3.

4. See Aquinas, *Summa Theologiae* 1.87.2–3.

5. "An act of willing is understood by the intellect both (a) insofar as someone perceives himself to be willing (*inquantum aliquis percipit se velle*) and also

Subjectivity in Contemporary Philosophy

Although Aquinas uses the term *person* to designate an individual reality with a special dignity, and even though he gives an account of how we come to have knowledge of our acts of knowing and willing and of our rational powers, his philosophical interests are not primarily concerned with what today we might call the self or the I. Modern and contemporary thought, on the other hand, are especially interested in the inner subjectivity of the human person. For them, the term *person* no longer designates a stable reality or substance that has the powers of reason and will. *Person* now emphasizes the inner reality of rational beings and their personal experience of freedom, self-determination, love, and intersubjectivity. It also highlights the unique gift that each person is, as well as the personal contribution that each person makes to the communities she forms a part of.

The more proximate origins of this emphasis on the interiority of the person and freedom can be found in German Romantic thought of the nineteenth century (Johann Gottlieb Fichte, Friedrich Wilhelm Joseph Schelling, Georg Wilhelm Friedrich Hegel) and in the writings of the Danish religious thinker Søren Kierkegaard, with his analysis of human existence as inwardness and subjectivity and the importance he gives to the individual and her experiences. Further developments that increase the focus on the person, especially with regard to freedom, come from important philosophical movements that arose in the early twentieth century. These include phenomenology (Edmund Husserl, Max Scheler, Dietrich von

(b) insofar as someone has cognition of the nature of this act (*inquantum aliquis cognoscit naturam huius actus*) and, as a result, cognition of the nature of its source (*principium*), which is either a habit or a power." Aquinas, *Summa Theologiae* 1.87.4.

Hildebrand, Edith Stein, Maurice Merleau-Ponty), existentialism (Martin Heidegger, Karl Jaspers, Jean-Paul Sartre, Simone de Beauvoir), and personalism (Emmanuel Mounier, Gabriel Marcel).[6]

Although these authors' views varied in many ways—many of them were Christian while others were agnostics or atheists—their thought and work strongly influenced twentieth-century philosophy and culture. This included Catholic intellectuals, whose contributions led to a re-evaluation, reinterpretation, and sometimes even reformulation of Thomistic philosophical thought. The following sections present three authors who represent diverse ways of rethinking Aquinas in dialogue with contemporary and theological considerations regarding the person.

Ratzinger: person as relation

In an article first published in 1973, Joseph Ratzinger reminds his readers that the notion of person is a product of Christian theology and that it "did not simply grow out of mere human philosophizing, but out of the interplay between philosophy and the antecedent given of faith."[7] More specifically, the concept of person arose from two questions: "What is God?" and "Who is Christ?" In the first section of this article, Ratzinger focuses on how the notion of person arose from the development of Trinitarian theology in the first four centuries of the Church and on how this relational understanding of the person

6. For a brief account of these contemporary trends in philosophy, see Mariano Fazio and Francisco Fernández Labastida, *A History of Contemporary Philosophy: Nineteenth and Twentieth Centuries* (New York: Scepter, 2011), parts 4 and 5.

7. Joseph Ratzinger, "Concerning the Notion of Person in Theology," trans. Michael Waldstein, *Communio* 17, no. 3 (Fall 1990), p. 439; originally published as "Zum Personenverständis in der Theologie," in *Dogma und Verkündigung* (Munich: Erich Wewel, 1973), pp. 205–223.

can also be used to illuminate not only the mystery of the Divine Trinity but also the human person.

In God, there are three Persons, and in this context person must be understood as *relation* and pure relatedness. If, in God, person means relation, this means that relation is not something superadded to the person but *is* the person itself.[8] In this case, states Ratzinger, person is "not a substance that closes itself in itself, but the phenomenon of complete relativity."[9]

Although the understanding of person as relation is at first only a statement about the Trinity, Ratzinger suggests that it can also refer to the human spirit. After further considerations about the development of the notion of person in Christology, he then puts forward a more detailed description of spirit that he believes can further our understanding of spirit in human beings. More concretely, *spirit as relation* is *capacity to know oneself and others*: "it is the nature of sprit to put itself in relation, the capacity to see itself and the other." This means that spirit "not only *is*, but reaches beyond itself, it comes to itself." In other words, "in transcending itself it *has* itself; by being with the other it first becomes itself, it comes to itself." Consequently, a person's fullness is not that of a self-sufficient substance that is closed in upon itself but rather involves a *going out of oneself to another*: "the nature of the spirit which comes to itself and actualizes its own fullness only by going away from itself, by going to what is other than itself."[10]

Wojtyła: the acting person

In the years leading up to his becoming Pope John Paul II, Karol Wojtyła's philosophical inquiries led him to investigate

8. See Ratzinger, "Person in Theology," p. 444.

9. Ratzinger, "Person in Theology," p. 445.

10. Ratzinger, "Person in Theology," p. 451.

how it could be possible to develop a philosophical anthropology that uncovers the structures of the inner subjectivity of the human being.[11] Such an anthropology would, in his view, supplement and expand the more classical "objective" approach to the human being as an individual of a rational substance.

The aim is to arrive at what Wojtyła calls the "irreducible" in man. This irreducible is described as "that which is originally or fundamentally human," as "what in every man is unique and unrepeatable," and as that through which the human person "is not just an individual of the species, but through which he is a person: a *subject*."[12]

To arrive at this inner reality of the human being, Wojtyła proposes a methodology that makes use of the human person's individual *lived experiences*. By focusing on these lived experiences instead of an objective ontological analysis of powers and operations, Wojtyła hopes to capture human subjectivity as an active dynamism or, to use the title of one of his later books, as an *acting person*.[13]

---

11. This section follows an article that develops a paper submitted to an international conference in Paris in June 1975, later published in Polish, and later still translated into English: Karol Wojtyła, "Subjectivity and 'the Irreducible' in Man," in *Person and Act and Related Essays*, trans. Grzegorz Ignatik (Washington DC: The Catholic University of America Press, 2021), pp. 536–545; originally published in Polish: "Podmiotowośći i 'to, co nieredukowalne' w człowieku," *Ethos* 1, nos. 2–3 (1988), pp. 21–28.

12. Wojtyła, "Subjectivity," pp. 537, 542.

13. "For it is a question not only of a metaphysical objectivization of man as the acting subject, that is, the agent of his acts, but also of a presentation of the person as the subject experiencing his acts, his experiences, and in all this, his subjectivity. Once such a demand is put forward in the interpretation of the acting man (*l'homme agissant*), the category of lived-experience must find its place in anthropology and ethics; moreover, to a certain degree it must stand in the center of respective interpretations." Wojtyła, "Subjectivity," p. 540.

Thus, starting with lived experience, we can have access to the concrete "I" as "a subject experiencing himself." Further analysis reveals structures that determine this concrete "I" (as person and as acting subject). More specifically, it reveals (a) the deepest dependencies of our acts and experiences in our own "I"; and (b) the personal dynamic structure of self-determination of "I" as one who possesses himself and is capable of governing himself.[14]

Having outlined an anthropology of subjectivity, Wojtyła then finishes his article with some considerations about how to further develop these insights within the context of the anthropological and ethical concerns and questions that arise in the contemporary world.

Polo: person as gift-love

Another proposal that expands Thomistic philosophical anthropology while at the same time engaging with modern and contemporary philosophy comes from the Spanish philosopher Leonardo Polo.

Although Polo accepts the Aristotelian-Thomistic anthropology that we have been studying as fundamentally correct, he, like Ratzinger and Wojtyła, believes that the modern and contemporary emphasis on the interiority and subjectivity of the human person contains valuable insights that can be integrated into a renewed or reforged Thomistically inspired philosophy. In this regard, Polo proposes going deeper into the study of the inner existence of the person. Like Aquinas, Polo recognizes that we exercise vital operations, and like Wojtyła, Polo is very much aware of the special character of our lived experience of acts of self-knowledge and freedom by which we possess and govern ourselves. This is

14. Wojtyła, "Subjectivity," pp. 541–542.

for Polo, as it was for Wojtyła, a clear indication of the personal and subjective dimension of the person and of human nature that sets human beings apart and distinguishes them from the natures and manner of existing of other, nonpersonal beings.

However, when it comes to understanding the inner core or intimacy from which acts of the intellect and will flow, Polo, like Ratzinger and Wojtyła, expresses dissatisfaction with the characterization of this reality as a substance. Instead of identifying this innermost core (which Polo calls *person* or *personal act of being*) as a fixed thing or completed substance that subsists in itself, Polo understands it first of all as an overflowing act. Here, by act, Polo means an existing that is much more than a vital operation executed by a power of the soul. In Polo's understanding, the powers and operations of the soul (which we studied in the first eight chapters of this book) are *manifestations* of a more profound, more radical act, which is the *intimacy* or *act of being of the person*.

Being a person is, therefore, not simply being a thing or being a substance (which then can perform operations). Instead, being-person means intimacy, inwardness, and overflowing activity. While Wojtyła identifies the subject of knowing and free acts as the *acting person*, Polo goes further and understands it to be *personal act of being*, an *act that is always more* (in Spanish, *además*). Throughout his writings, Polo describes this personal act in various ways: co-existence, being-additionally, intellectual light, transcendental freedom, and personal gift-love. While a complete overview of Polo's philosophical anthropology is not possible here, we will, in this section, offer an outline of his understanding of the person as gift-love.

To understand the person as gift-love, we should go back to our discussion of what the will is. For Aquinas, the will is the rational appetite, and as such, it is the power to tend toward something or some action that reason has judged to be good. When presented with some good, the will can tend toward it, and it does so in the form of an affection of the will. We also saw how this can take the form of freely intending an end, freely choosing a means, and enjoying the possession of that end.

Note that from this perspective, the will is either tending to a good that it does not yet possess (giving rise to the affections of love and desire) or it is resting in a good or end that it has achieved and possesses (giving rise to the affection of joy). This applies to all particular goods (like eating pepperoni pizza, watching a movie, or spending time with Grandma) and also to the final end (happiness). The will, in this sense, is about moving toward goods that it desires and then resting in and enjoying that good when it is possessed.

Polo, however, proposes that because the person is act (one that overflows and *is-additionally*), it follows that its manifestation in acts of the will cannot be limited to satisfying desires for goods. If the person is overflowing act, then this should be made manifest in acts of the will by which the person *gives*, *contributes*, and *brings something new into the world*.[15] Furthermore, insofar as gift involves a giving that is accepted, gift requires someone who *gives* and another who *accepts*.[16] Without giving, there is no gift. But it is also true that without accepting there is no gift either. For example, if I try to give my mother beautiful flowers on her birthday, but there is no one at home

15. See Leonardo Polo, *Having, Giving, Hoping*, trans. Roderrick Esclanda and Alberto I. Vargas (South Bend, IN: Leonardo Polo Institute of Philosophy Press, 2023), p. 43.

16. For a theory of gift in cultural practices and art, see Lewis Hyde, *The Gift: Creativity and the Artist in the Modern World* (New York: Vintage Books, 2007), pp. xv–xxiii and 3–31; and Makoto Fujimura, *Art and Faith: A Theology of Making* (New Haven, CT: Yale University Press, 2020), pp. 1–39.

to accept them, then those flowers have not yet become a gift. But if my mother is at home and accepts my giving her flowers, then the flowers become a beautiful, personal gift.

In Polo's anthropology, giving and accepting involve acts of the will that go beyond mere desire for goods and satisfaction when we possess them. Also, aside from being acts of the will, giving and receiving reveal a personal reality that is deeper and more intimate than the will (and reason)—a reality that, as we have been seeing, Polo identifies as the intimacy that the person is, a personal act of being that is ever overflowing.[17]

Finally, insofar as giving and accepting on the level of the will is a manifestation of this more profound intimate activity, we can say that the intimacy and personal act of being that is the person is also a giving and accepting, but one that exists on a deeper, personal level. As such, person as overflowing act is revealed as an act that is gift-love and the source of acts of giving and accepting on the level of the will.

SUMMARY

1. For Aquinas, a person is an individual substance of a rational nature.
2. For Aquinas, the first operation of the intellect is simple apprehension by which we know the essence of material things. The intellect is not known by abstraction or simple apprehension.

17. "But gifting also implies that human nature is now defined differently (and not in contradiction or in opposition to, nor even in concordance with Greek anthropology). Man is not ultimately defined—or solely defined—as the being capable of having, since it is necessary to find the root of his capacity for giving. The principle of gifting has to be more radical than immanence and even virtue. This is what is called intimacy." Polo, *Having, Giving, Hoping*, p. 45.

3. When the intellect is knowing, it can then know its own operation, itself as the principle of operation, and the intellectual habits that it has.
4. Modern and contemporary philosophical anthropology focuses its attention on the interiority (or subjectivity) of the human person.
5. Ratzinger proposes applying the theological origin of the notion of person as relation to the human person. Person as relation is characterized by relation to oneself and knowledge of and relationship with others.
6. Wojtyła proposes a methodology that uses lived experience to discover the structures of human subjectivity. This reveals the irreducible in man, which is understood as an acting person.
7. Polo proposes an anthropology of the human person as gift-love that manifests itself in giving and accepting.

CHAPTER 10

Manifestations of the Person

In the 1997 Danish film, *Babette's Feast*, Babette Hersant one day wins the lottery. She decides to use the money she won to create a "real French dinner" for the residents of the tiny Danish village where she has been living for the past fourteen years. For this dinner to become a reality, Babette first arranges for her nephew to gather supplies and ingredients from Paris, then she prepares the meal herself. Meanwhile, as the villagers become aware of what is about to take place, they make a pact with each other to make no mention of the food during the meal, and to not speak of any pleasure that comes from it. When the dinner does happen, a series of reactions from guests break down their resolve, and a festive atmosphere begins to reign, in which suspicions and fears from the past are overcome in a sort of festive redemption.

The theme of gift and of the giving and accepting that makes gifts possible is present in this film on many levels. It also shows us an important dimension of the anthropological structure of the human person: namely, that the gift-love of the human person manifests itself in acts of giving that are then accepted by others (who, in turn, themselves give to others). This manifesting of the person (of gift-love) in actions is the topic of this final chapter.

Person and Manifestation

In chapters 1 through 8, we learned the basic outlines of classical Aristotelian-Thomistic philosophical anthropology. This anthropology is based on a philosophy of nature that places substance (being that subsists in itself) at its center. It characterizes man as a kind of bodily substance, one that is alive (animated by a soul), with powers or capabilities to carry out a variety of vital operations. Man is, more specifically, an animal with *logos* (reason), and thus capable of knowing truth and directing himself freely to his end. In this context, person is described as an individual *substance* of a rational nature.

In chapter 9, we considered more contemporary approaches to the human person. These perspectives pay much closer attention to the intimacy or subjectivity of the person. One example of how to approach this subjectivity is Wojtyła's phenomenologically inspired analysis of lived experience, which reveals the irreducible subject of human action as an underlying act that he describes as the *acting person*. Ratzinger, for his part, suggests an understanding of human beings that draws upon the theological origins of the concept of person: one that sees the person not so much as a closed-in substance but as a *relation* with oneself that opens up to others. Finally, we took a look at Polo's proposal, in which he characterizes the deepest intimacy of the human person as overflowing act that is gift-love.

This final chapter expands upon the insights of contemporary thought touched upon in the previous chapter and offers a proposal about how they can enrich Aristotelian-Thomistic philosophical anthropology with new light and direction. The chapter is generally ordered around specific themes that parallel those already covered in the discussion of Aquinas' philosophical anthropology (chapters 1–8), but with additional perspectives that stem from how these themes are enriched and expanded by the contemporary insights of Ratzinger, Wojtyła, and Polo. Another way to view how this chapter is organized is to see it as being inspired by Polo's understanding of the person's intimacy as overflowing activity that is gift-love, which then manifests itself through human nature as described by Aquinas (unity of body and soul, powers, habits, and operations).

This is obviously just one possible (though personal) way of looking at the human person. As mentioned above, it follows themes already present in Aquinas, but attempts to see them in the light of proposals set forth by Polo. Its exposition is thus inspired by Polo (along with a few points from other authors) yet not simply a straightforward exposition Polo's thought.[1]

Being-in-the-World

Use

My ordinary existence takes place in a world of things, and I ordinarily use these things in a routine manner, without much thought as to what they are and how they are related to other things. I am, for example, at this moment writing with a purple gel pen (an EverGel pen from Pentel, to be exact). Although I am now consciously thinking about the pen, thinking about it is not my normal way of relating to it. What I normally do with the pen is that I *use* it for writing. As I use it to write, I am focused on the writing and not consciously reflecting on how the pen works. Nor do I pay much attention to the pen

1. For a more in-depth treatment of these topics from a perspective more directly in line with Polo's works, see Juan Fernando Sellés, *Antropología Para Inconformes* (Madrid: Rialp, 2006).

itself. I could, of course, turn my attention to the pen, to how smoothly it writes and to the beautiful purple color of its ink, but those are not the usual, ordinary ways that I relate to the pen. The ordinary relationship I have with my pen is that of *using* it for writing.

But writing (with a pen) requires other things, other objects, like paper, for example. So, as I write, I also relate to the paper. And just as it was with the pen, my relationship to the paper is normally that of using it, without paying much attention to special considerations such as what paper is or where it comes from.

So, when I write, I *use* pen and I *use* paper. And thus, within my ordinary existence, if I ask, What is a pen? or What is paper? the answer isn't a description of the physical characteristics and properties of pen and paper. The answer, instead, is that a pen is an instrument for writing, and paper is another instrument related to writing—in this case, a surface that can be written upon.

Instrumental plexus and world

We can follow Polo (who in this analysis is inspired by Heidegger) even further along this line. Aside from my relating to pen and to paper as I use them for writing, pen and paper are also *related to each other* within the activity of writing. That is, a pen has meaning as a pen only insofar as it is related to other instruments together with which it forms part of the activity of writing. In fact, if we pull back a little and look at writing from a broader perspective, we realize that it involves many more instruments, all of which are related to each other: gel pens, ball pens, fountain pens, felt-tip pens, markers, highlighters, white paper, pink paper, black paper, thick paper, thin paper, rough paper, smooth paper, stationery, teal-colored journal notebooks, paper clips, Japanese mechanical pencils, and so forth. And beyond that, we can see that writing itself is related to many other activities, such as teaching, leisure reading, bookstores, author book signings, and book publishing.

All these activities and the tools and instruments that form part of them constitute an intertwining web of activities and instruments that Polo calls an *instrumental plexus*. Taken as a whole, the various interconnected networks of activities and tools that we engage with in our ordinary lives form the *world* in which human persons exist.[2] Human existence can then, at least in part, be initially understood as the mode of existence of persons as they engage in the activities and use the various instruments that collectively constitute the world in which they exist. In other words, this initial practical dimension of human existence can be described as *being-in-the-world*.

World, then, does not refer simply to the various natural substances that spatially exist around us. Instead, the world that surrounds us and of which we form a part is constituted by the tools and activities that we ourselves bring about.

Newness and novelty

This characterization of human existence as being-in-the-world is similar to Aquinas' account of practical reason and making, but adds to it in significant ways.

One such way is the emphasis that Heidegger and Polo give to the interrelatedness that instruments and activities have with each other. Aquinas focuses mostly on the activities of making specific things and on the crafts that arise from them. But,

2. See Polo, *Having, Giving, Hoping*, pp. 10–20.

although he mentions how one craft might be subordinated to another, he does not go into detail about how they are related to each other in an instrumental plexus or world in which human beings exist.

A more substantial difference concerns *why* human beings go about these activities and *how* they manifest the richness of the human person. For Aquinas, human beings make things (with their hands and reason) first to provide for their basic needs and then to live well. But from the perspective of an understanding of the person as gift-love, practical activity can be understood more as a manifestation of the richness and creative activity of the human person. For Polo, the person is overflowing activity that manifests itself in practical activity as bringing newness and novelty into the world. Thus, although much of what we make is for survival and to meet our needs, insofar as our activities flow from a source of gift-love they always involve an element of novelty.

The tools within an instrumental plexus receive their very meaning as tools from the creative activity of persons. Many thousands of years ago, for example, someone picked up a stick and realized that it could be used to make markings in the dirt. Over time, generations of creative persons developed writing systems. Then, others discovered they could use small twigs to write on clay tablets. Eventually, some other person (probably with the help of others) came up with the idea that led to the invention of gel pens and, in collaboration with others (who had discovered how to make purple ink), brought purple gel pens into the world. At each step of the path leading to purple gel pens, not only was there a need to be met but there were also creative acts that brought something new into the world, something that would never have come into existence without the creative gift of persons.

An understanding of the person as gift-love that overflows and manifests itself in practical action thus introduces a new perspective to our conception of work and our ordinary existence. Work is now no longer just an activity necessary for our survival, nor is it simply aimed at producing goods for mass consumption or individual personal gain. Instead, work is a manifestation of creative personal activity that gives something *new* to the world and to the persons that exist in that world. Insofar as this giving is accepted and continued by persons and made into new giving, the world that we exist in becomes one that is constituted by the giving and accepting of gifts.[3] This creative point of view also has repercussions on how we understand our relationships to the material cosmos (ecology),[4] as well as how we organize and conceive the driving motivations and goals of our economic activity.[5]

Being-with-persons

Being-in-the-world—that is, being engaged in activities of giving and accepting within an instrumental plexus—involves not just using tools for activities but also encountering other

3. Polo, *Having, Giving, Hoping*, pp. 39–50.

4. See, for example, Pope Francis: "An inadequate presentation of Christian anthropology gave rise to a wrong understanding of the relationship between human beings and the world. Often, what was handed on was a Promethean vision of mastery over the world, which gave the impression that the protection of nature was something that only the faint-hearted cared about. Instead, our 'dominion' over the universe should be understood more properly in the sense of responsible stewardship." Francis, Encyclical Letter on Care for our Common Home *Laudato si'* (March 24, 2015), no. 116, Vatican website: www.vatican.va.

5. See, for example Polo's suggestion that the economy should be motivated by entrepreneurs who want to give instead of by consumer demand. Leonardo Polo, *Rich and Poor: Equality and Inequality*, trans. Roderrick Esclanda and Mark Mannion (South Bend, IN: Leonardo Polo Institute of Philosophy Press, 2017), p. 23.

persons. It is in these encounters with persons that real gifts appear. We saw earlier how human persons contribute to the world through generous, creative acts that bring innovation. But, for these acts truly to be gifts, they need to be accepted, and accepting is an action of a person. In *Babette's Feast*, Babette does not limit herself to bringing French cuisine to Denmark in general. What she really wants is to give a gift to each one of the residents of her village. But for her dinner to be a gift, it must be actively accepted by her dinner guests. This accepting cannot simply be a mindless consumption of food either. If Babette's dinner is truly to be a gift, it must be personally accepted by each one of her guests, and this entails not just a spiritual accepting by the will but also an accepting of the sensory pleasures that the excellent food and the beautiful preparation and presentation produce in each of the guests.

If giving is to become gift, it needs the accepting of another person. Giving thus requires personally thinking of the person to whom the giving is directed (at least to some extent). And on the other side, accepting involves some sort of knowledge that the giving is offered as a gift from another person. A teacup placed on a dining-room table with its handle at three o'clock, for example, can be a personal giving if it is done thinking of the person who will sit at that setting and when it is done from a personal desire to give that gift. Similarly, accepting the gift of the teacup's position entails some sort of recognition of the personal gift being given.[6]

6. See Leonardo Polo, *Persona y Libertad* (Pamplona: Eunsa, 2017), p. 75, where he discusses how difficult it is to gift someone a tie. For this particular example of the teacup, see Rebecca Leigh Sullivan, "Bearing Witness to the Personal Core of Teaching" (PhD diss., Columbia University, 2023), pp. 118, 141–146, and 198–199, https://doi.org/10.7916/xk7a-aj02.

Embodiment

Another consequence of conceiving human existence as being-in-the-world is how we view our bodies. The fact that my experience of ordinary existence is that of *already* being-in-the-world (that is, I experience myself as already being-in-the-world before I consciously reflect upon this fact) means that my first experience of the world is that I am already practically engaging with things and persons in the world before I think about them. This, in turn, means that my initial engagement with the world is not through abstract operations of my intellect but by my experiencing the world through my body. My body, therefore, is not seen as a separate thing or object of experience. Nor is my body experienced as something different from me. Rather, my body is *that part of me by which I experience the world and through which I am in the world*.

In addition to this, insofar as I intervene in the world and bring something new to it through my creative action, I do so through my body (and other faculties of my human nature). Once again, my body is not a separate thing that I interact with, nor is it just another instrument along with others that I use in the world. Instead, my body is a *manifestation* of my person as gift-love, through which I can engage in giving and accepting.[7]

This, in turn, gives us a more positive sense of *gender*. The fact that we are embodied beings that are either male or female also affects how the gift-love of the person is manifested in giving and accepting in *masculine* or *feminine* ways.[8] Seen in this

---

7. "*The human body* in its visible dynamic is *the terrain and, in a sense, even the means of expression for the person.*" Karol Wojtyła, "Integration and Somaticity," in *Person and Act and Related Essays*, p. 312.

8. See Jutta Burggraf, *¿Qué quiere decir género? Un nuevo modo de hablar* (San José, Costa Rica: Promesa, 2001).

light, manifesting myself in my masculinity or femininity is far from being a limiting factor; instead, it is an aspect of myself that I can take up and make a vehicle for manifesting the gift-love that I am.

Affectivity

Giving and accepting as an embodied being in the world suggests a number of ways of examining human affectivity.

Recall that in chapter 4 we studied sensible appetites and their passions. In that context, love is the first passion that arises in the sense appetite when something has been evaluated by the estimative power to be suitable for the organism. Then, in chapter 6, we saw that the will has affections that parallel those of the sensible appetites but are applied to the rational appetite, which is the will. Here, love means the first inclination toward something or some action that the practical intellect has understood to be good (and which, therefore, in some way, leads to happiness).

Now, in the light of the person as gift-love who gives and accepts through her human nature (her body and the powers of the soul that we have been studying), a dimension of human affectivity appears, one that involves interactions between persons as they give and accept. Though there is no definitive list of these affections, we can call to mind feelings of acceptance or rejection, the feelings that come with friendship, those involving indifference or exclusion, and so on. They may also be more typically masculine or feminine affections. Other examples are love as attraction, desire, goodwill, or marital love.[9] All these involve attempts at manifesting

9. See Karol Wojtyła, *Love and Responsibility,* trans. H. T. Willetts (New York: Farrar, Straus and Giroux, 1981), pp. 73–100.

personal gift-love through actions of giving and accepting, attempts that can either fail (through a defect in the giving or in its not being accepted) or succeed.

God and Transcendence

For most of this chapter, we have been dwelling on how the person (one's subjectivity or intimacy) as gift-love manifests herself through her human nature, that is, through acts of the will by which she gives and accepts. We now need to look more closely at the person herself as gift-love, and not just in her manifestations through acts of giving and accepting through powers of her nature.

What is gift-love? In the last chapter, we saw how contemporary philosophy often avoids characterizing the person as substance, and instead seeks to understand person more as relation or as act. We also saw that, in the case of Polo, one of the ways he understands the person is as gift-love. Throughout this chapter, we explored how this gift-love *manifests* itself in acts of giving and accepting. Gift-love, however, is not identical to these manifestations of the person. So, if gift-love is not a substance, and if it is not one of its manifestations as acts of giving and accepting, then what is it? According to Polo, this gift-love is also a *giving* and an *accepting*, but not on the level of acts of the will. Instead, it has to do with the giving and accepting of the reality of gift-love itself. Now, since gift-love is the person (innermost intimacy and subjectivity), this question concerns *the very giving and accepting of the person that I am*; that is, of the *who* that I am. But who gives me the who that I am? The answer can only be God. God gives me my personal existence (my who) and, to the extent that I accept the who that I am, I am a gift of God.

And what does it mean that I accept who I am? According to Polo, I accept God's gift of who I am by the acts of giving that we have described above—through my nature, including body and acts of the will by which I give and the acts by which I grow in virtue—but as directed to God in the hope of being accepted by him.

SUMMARY

1. As being-in-the-world, the human person uses tools.
2. The human person gives or endows tools with their meaning within different activities.
3. Tools and activities interconnect with other tools and activities to form an instrumental plexus.
4. The multiple instrumental plexuses that we are engaged with constitute the world in which we exist.
5. Human persons can thus be described as being-in-the-world.
6. Persons as gift-love manifest themselves through acts of creative giving that bring something new into the world.
7. Persons as gift-love establish relationships of mutual giving and accepting with other persons.
8. Being embodied is part of being-in-the-world.
9. Gender (being a man or being a woman) is a dimension of being an embodied being-in-the-world.
10. Being embodied affects how the gift-love that I am manifests itself in acts of giving and accepting.
11. Human affectivity includes feelings that arise from interactions with other persons in relationships of giving and accepting.

12. The unique characteristics of each person's human nature can be integrated by the person in such a way that they become personalized ways of the person's manifesting herself through giving and accepting.
13. On the level of person, gift-love is accepting the person that I am, which God gives, by giving through actions with the hope of being accepted.

CONCLUSION

I am now writing this page with black ink. My purple gel pen died last night as I was writing chapter 10, and it was the last of a whole pack of purple pens, all of which have now run out of ink, victims (or instruments) of my writing this book.

Does this mean that the writing of this book has come to an end? Or does my new pen color promise a new beginning? Or does it demand a rewriting of the book (now in a new color)?

What is more likely is that the time has come to conclude, but not end.

A tradition followed by Marvel superhero movies is that the end credits include brief scenes, either in the middle of the credits, or at the end, or both. These scenes sometimes allude to some side character who appeared earlier in the film. At other times, they give a taste of future films to come.

This conclusion is like one of those end-credit scenes. It is both an occasion to look back at what we have covered and an opportunity to take a look around and get a sense of where we want to go from here.

In the introduction, we asked, "What is a human being?" We also asked, "Who am I?"

The first eight chapters gave us an answer to the first question: *a human being is a rational animal*. There, we learned the basic outline of Aristotelian-Thomistic philosophical anthropology: living beings as a substantial unity of body and soul, the powers and operations of living beings, the notion of habits, and the ultimate goal of human life, which is happiness.

In the last two chapters, we took a more contemporary approach, with an emphasis on understanding the interiority of the human person as relation and gift-love. We sought out the answer to the second question (*Who* am I?). The answer to this question is, however, not quite as simple as it may seem. We could, of course, simply end with this answer: *I am gift-love*. That would be a nice answer with which we could end this book. But it certainly doesn't conclude it. Although it is true that the answer to the question about who I am can be "I am gift-love," it leaves out one crucial reality, namely the "I." To answer the question "Who am I?" with "I am gift-love" risks giving a generic answer to a personal question. The question "Who am I?" is a personal question about my own personal "I," about who I am in my intimacy, in my subjectivity, and this question is not adequately answered by a generic description of an "I."

The more proper response to the question about who I am requires a revelation of my personal intimacy. And so, even though it is correct *in general* to say that I am gift-love, a more profound response would require a more personal understanding of *the personal gift-love that I am*. This gift-love, as we have seen, manifests itself in actions of giving and accepting. And, insofar as these actions are my own personal actions, it is through and in them that *who I am* manifests itself. Thus, the only way to truly know *who* I am is through my acts of giving and accepting. And the only way for me to know *who* you are is through your acts of giving, which I accept, and through your acts of accepting what I am giving you.

In brief, I come to know *who* you are, and you come to know *who* I am when we successfully exchange gifts that manifest who we are.

But, of course, the one who truly knows completely *who I am* and *who you are* is God.

But that is the subject of another story.

BIBLIOGRAPHY

Works by Aristotle and Thomas Aquinas

Aquinas, Thomas. *Aristotle:* On Interpretation; *Commentary by St. Thomas and Cajetan*. Translated by Jean T. Oesterle. Milwaukee, WI: Marquette University Press, 1962.

———. *Commentary on Aristotle's* De anima. Translated by Kenelm Foster, OP and Sylvester Humphries, OP. New Haven: Yale University Press, 1951.

———. *Commentary on Aristotle's* Politics. Translated by Ernest L. Fortin and Peter D. O'Neill. "Sententia libri Politicorum." St. Isidore E-book Library. https://isidore.co/aquinas/Politics.htm.

———. *Commentary on the* Nichomachean Ethics. 2 vols. Translated by C. I. Litzinger, OP. Chicago: Regnery, 1964.

———. *Commentary on the* Posterior Analytics *of Aristotle*. Translated by Fabian R. Larcher, OP. Albany, NY: Magi Books, 1970.

———. *Summa Theologiae*. Translated by Alfred J. Freddoso. "New English Translation of St. Thomas Aquinas' *Summa Theologiae* (*Summa Theologica*)." Updated July 11, 2023. https://www3.nd.edu/~afreddos/summa-translation/TOC.htm.

Aristotle. *De anima*. Translated by C. D. C. Reeve (Indianapolis, IN: Hackett, 2017).

Works by Contemporary Thinkers

Polo, Leonardo. *Having, Giving, Hoping*. Translated by Roderrick Esclanda and Alberto I. Vargas. South Bend, IN: Leonardo Polo Institute of Philosophy Press, 2023.

———. *Persona y Libertad*. Pamplona: Eunsa, 2017.

———. *Rich and Poor: Equality and Inequality*. Translated by Roderrick Esclanda and Mark Mannion. South Bend, IN: Leonardo Polo Institute of Philosophy Press, 2017.

Ratzinger, Joseph. "Concerning the Notion of Person in Theology." Translated by Michael Waldstein. *Communio* 17, no. 3 (Fall 1990): 439–454. Originally published as "Zum Personenverständis in der Theologie." In *Dogma und Verkündigung,* 205–223. Munich: Erich Wewel, 1973.

Wojtyła, Karol. *Love and Responsibility*. Translated by H. T. Willetts. New York: Farrar, Straus and Giroux, 1981.

———. *Person and Act and Related Essays*. Translated by Grzegorz Ignatik. Washington, DC: The Catholic University of America Press, 2021.

Other Works Used

Brock, Stephen L. *The Philosophy of Thomas Aquinas: A Sketch*. Eugene, OR: Wipf and Stock, 2015.

Burggraf, Jutta. *¿Qué quiere decir género? Un nuevo modo de hablar*. San José, Costa Rica: Promesa, 2001.

Confucius. *The Analects of Confucius*. Translated by A. Charles Muller. "The Analects of Confucius 論語." Revised December 1, 2021. http://www.acmuller.net/con-dao/analects.html.

Dolensek, Nate et al. "Facial Expressions of Emotion States and Their Neuronal Correlates in Mice." *Science* 368, no. 6486 (April 3, 2020): 89–94. https://www.science.org/doi/10.1126/science.aaz9468.

Fazio, Mariano, and Francisco Fernández Labastida. *A History of Contemporary Philosophy: Nineteenth and Twentieth Centuries*. New York: Scepter, 2011.

Francis. Encyclical Letter on Care for our Common Home *Laudato si'*. May 24, 2015. Vatican website: www.vatican.va.

Fujimura, Makoto. *Art and Faith: A Theology of Making*. New Haven, CT: Yale University Press, 2020.

Hyde, Lewis. *The Gift: Creativity and the Artist in the Modern World*. New York: Vintage Books, 2007.

Plato. *Protagoras*. Translated by Stanley Lombardo and Karen Bell. In *Plato: Complete Works,* 746–790. Edited by John M. Cooper. Indianapolis: Hackett, 1997.

Sellés, Juan Fernando. *Antropología Para Inconformes*. Madrid: Rialp, 2006.

Sokolowski, Robert. "Soul and the Transcendence of the Human Person." In *Christian Faith and Human Understanding: Studies on the Eucharist, Trinity, and the Human Person,* 151–164. Washington, DC: The Catholic University of America Press, 2006.

Sullivan, Rebecca Leigh. "Bearing Witness to the Personal Core of Teaching." PhD diss., Columbia University, 2023. https://doi.org/10.7916/xk7a-aj02.

ACKNOWLEDGMENTS

A work like this can only come about through the help of countless acts of encouragement and inspiration from a great variety of persons—some known, others quietly working in a hidden way. Nevertheless, an attempt can still be made to acknowledge those whose patient assistance and collaboration have been more directly evident. Thus, my gratitude to Scepter Publishers and their staff, especially to Meredith Koopman, who has so diligently accompanied this book's gestation. My thanks also to Larry Olsen, who read through the drafts of this work and made several very helpful suggestions. And finally, I would like to express my gratitude to the staffs of Darien Study Center, Arnold Hall, and Shellbourne Conference Center for their gift of creating a home where projects like this little book can find the inspiration and nourishment they need to come to life and flourish.